TRAINING
SOURCES

Outdoor Training

TRAINING
SOURCES

Outdoor Training

book of activities

BILL KROUWEL
STEVE GOODWILL

Viva Books
New Delhi | Mumbai | Chennai | Kolkata | Bangalore | Hyderabad | Kochi

First published as "Training Activities: Outdoor Training"

This edition published in 2009
Reprinted 2010

VIVA BOOKS PRIVATE LIMITED

- 4737/23 Ansari Road, Daryaganj, New Delhi 110 002
  E-mail: vivadelhi@vivagroupindia.net, Tel. 42242200
- 76, Service Industries, Shirvane, Sector 1, Nerul, Navi Mumbai 400 706
  E-mail: vivamumbai@vivagroupindia.net, Tel. 27721273, 27721274
- Jamals Fazal Chambers, 26 Greams Road, Chennai 600 006
  E-mail: vivachennai@vivagroupindia.net, Tel. 28290304, 28294241
- B-103, Jindal Towers, 21/1A/3 Darga Road, Kolkata 700 017
  E-mail: vivakolkata@vivagroupindia.net, Tel. 22836381, 22816713
- 7, Sovereign Park Apartments, 56-58, K. R. Road, Basavanagudi, Bangalore 560 004
  E-mail: vivabangalore@vivagroupindia.net, Tel. 26607409, 26607410
- 101-102 Mughal Marc Apartments, 3-4-637 to 641, Narayanguda, Hyderabad 500 029
  E-mail: vivahyderabad@vivagroupindia.net, Tel. 27564481, 27564482
- Beevi Towers, First Floor, SRM Road, Kaloor, Kochi 682 018, Kerala
  E-mail: vivakochi@vivagroupindia.net, Tel: 0484-2403055, 2403056
- 232, GNB Road, Beside UCO Bank, Silpukhuri, Guwahati 781 003
  E-mail: vivaguwahati@vivagroupindia.net, Tel: 0361-2666386

www.vivagroupindia.com

Published by arrangement with

Kogan Page Limited
120 Pentonville Road
London, N1 9JN, UK

ISBN: 978-81-309-1064-2

Published by Vinod Vasishtha for Viva Books Private Limited, 4737/23, Ansari Road, Daryaganj, New Delhi - 110 002. Printed and bound by Raj Press, R-3, Inderpuri, New Delhi - 110 012.

M0000 / M0453

Contents

Acknowledgements

The roots of some of the outdoor exercises in this book are now impossible to trace. Someone somewhere had a bright idea and as a result many others – ourselves included – over many years adopted, adapted and often transformed exercises to meet particular needs. What we have written is therefore sometimes completely our own work and sometimes the end-result of a process which involved us at later stages but may have started somewhere else.

We therefore acknowledge the contribution made by a host of anonymous development trainers over the years and thank them for initiating what has become a folk-process of change by degrees.

In some cases we were members of teams that originated particular exercises, and we are thus able to thank the following for their contributions, sometimes to exercise design, sometimes to the thought process that led to exercise design: Barry Aiken, Richard Bartrop, Chris Creswick, Roy Davies, Tony Hendry, John Herbert, Joe Jaina, Ralph Lewis, Paul Leedell, Chris Parker, Barry Peel, Andrew Perkins, Adrian Stabler, Phil Wright, Pete Willance, Roy Williams, John Campbell, Ray Birt, Cyril Levicki, and Alan Cattell, and Sue Bennett.

Permission to reproduce copyrighted work was freely given by Silva (UK) Ltd.

Help on technical matters was given by Dave Baines of Peak Training Services, Peter March of Derwent Outdoor Pursuits, and Robin Sermon.

Real appreciation is also due to our long-suffering wives and children who knew when to leave us alone, and to the thousands of course members who found themselves actually performing exercises contained herein.

Any mistakes are our own.

CHAPTER 1

THE OUTDOORS AND HOW TO USE IT FOR MANAGEMENT DEVELOPMENT

INTRODUCTION

Although this book is intended as a handbook of exercises, we felt when compiling it that we would be failing in our duty if we did not spend some time examining ways in which to use the outdoors for Management Development.

In this short chapter we thus examine:

- the need to match outdoor tasks to the people doing them, in terms of participants' physical, psychological and managerial needs;
- the need to ensure that outdoor exercises and programmes are relevant to the needs of delegates and their organizations;
- the need at all times to ensure physical and psychological safety in exercises and programmes.

MATCHING REAL TASKS TO REAL PEOPLE

A matter of physique

Managers come in all shapes and sizes. Like everyone else, as time passes, some become less physically fit whilst others retain the trimness of their youth. It is salutary to note that Joan Collins and Mollie Sugden are of similar age, whilst Jimmy Knapp shares his year of birth with Cliff Richard – and all belong to an age-group that might feasibly attend an outdoor management programme.

Failure to understand that a wide range of physical abilities exists in most management groups attending outdoor programmes can lead to:

- accidents and injuries – especially when delegates have been 'fired-up' to go a task too far;
- resentment and rejection of potential learning.

We therefore strongly recommend that exercises should match participants' physical abilities. In order to help you in this we have chosen exercises ranging from those in which delegates merely have to step a few yards from their (chauffeur-driven) transport, through to some which require a fairly high level of physical commitment.

In recognition of the wide range of physical ability, many of the exercises provide roles for a variety of physiques.

A matter of pressure

Even the least physically testing tasks can become onerous if too many are crammed into each day. We therefore recommend that every course contains about a 50:50 ratio of physical tasks to non-physical activity such as review and input. Circumstances may alter cases – for example, it may be that people need to learn lessons about handling pressure – so the 50:50 ratio is merely a guideline. Certainly, we found when working with unemployed young people in the early Eighties that full days helped build that all-important self-esteem. But even in those circumstances we learned to alternate tasks of high and low physicality.

We look back with very mixed feelings on some of our early management programmes, when delegates scuttled from task to task with hardly time to draw breath. We know that they learned much, but we have a horrible feeling that more was lost in the rush.

Trainers often feel a pressure to stuff outdoor programmes with activity in ways which they would never do on indoor courses. We do not know precisely why this should be, but it's an observable phenomenon, and one which is not helpful to true development in the long run. One very negative result is the propagation of myths by delegates, who often talk at great length about the activities but not much about review. The resulting folklore tends to be about people dangling upside-down over cliffs or 'gripping-up' in a cave, or suffering exhaustion from a hard walk in the forest, and can have a very negative effect on subsequent delegates.

If such nervousness is likely to be present, we recommend:

- a relaxed introductory session or (even better) pre-course briefing, in which it is explained that outdoor exercises are an integral part of a wider process and not an end in themselves;
- a policy of never putting pressure on people to undertake particular tasks. We go to the extent of making all tasks voluntary. So far, we have only experienced positive effects from this;
- in the introductory session we often talk of our shared fear of crawling creatures with too many legs, and the feelings we would experience if put in a room containing many such 'nasties'. We then draw the parallel with the fear that many feel when confronted with enclosed spaces, water or heights, and point out the negative results of forcing people into such situations;
- a policy of discouraging delegates from putting pressure on each other. This is particularly necessary when 'gung-ho' managers are in the same team as subordinates. We never hesitate to intervene when we see such pressure being applied;
- using outdoor safety staff who have sufficient maturity in outlook to support and enforce the above policies.

A matter of relevance

Sadly, outdoor providers exist who run standardized programmes for all comers. This is a pity because, just as participants come physically and psychologically in all shapes and sizes, managers' and organizations' needs vary greatly.

The outdoors is a very flexible medium indeed, and exercises and programmes can be put together which quite tightly address a very wide range of needs. For example, we have seen outdoor exercises which provoked learning in such specific and diverse areas as customer service and manufacturing reorganization.

We therefore recommend that exercises and the programmes of which they are a part should be tailored to the actual needs of the delegates and the organization.

A matter of process reality

The key to making outdoor programmes really relevant is to ensure that the tasks provoke the relevant processes. In the customer service exercise mentioned above, some of the delegates took the role of customers. As such they soon found themselves being patronized, hoodwinked, and bullied by the other delegates (organized into two competing 'suppliers') they experienced the inevitable feelings, and quite forcibly shared these in review. The lesson was salutary to all concerned, and the group was very open to guidance on how better to treat customers. Having received it, when the task restarted the group was able to translate the advice into behaviour. Mistakes were still made, but the *process reality* of the customers' experience was the key to the quantum shift in attitudes which resulted.

To help you choose tasks which provoke the appropriate process reality, we have included a matrix which matches exercises with development needs. See pages 55–56.

SAFETY

As well as issues related to the physique of delegates, there is the matter of safety in general. This is a most vital area, and one on which no effort should be spared.

In acknowledgement of this we have included specialized safety notes for underground, navigation, cliff-face, water-based and scaffolding exercises. (See Chapter 4.) Other exercises have their own sections on safety.

Safety notes

These should be issued on every occasion when the relevant exercises are being used, and their provisions should be observed by course staff as well as delegates. Further, staff should maintain a high level of vigilance at all times whenever groups are working on outdoor tasks. Even the weather needs to be watched – we recall a task involving long steel scaffold poles, which was proceeding perfectly safely until thunder and lightning began erupting around us. Our only course – which we immediately took – was to abandon the exercise and move indoors until the atmospherics abated.

One of the advantages of outdoor exercises, especially those involving cliffs or caves, is that they enable delegates to address fears and find ways of facing them. This is good for, among other things, promoting assertiveness. If, however, the gap between the delegate's fear and his or her will to overcome it is too great, undue social pressure can be a very negative thing, causing the delegate to feel isolated and inadequate. Unless you want people to feel like this (and we can think of no circumstances where this would be desirable) you should ensure that such pressure is avoided.

It may be that your judgement tells you that the gap is not too wide. In this case, it is sometimes helpful to provide a little private encouragement to the delegates concerned, but *always* leave them the choice as to whether to do the task or not. Often, giving time to think about it whilst doing some other necessary task helps. We find that kindness, reassurance and sympathy are much more helpful than ridicule and scorn.

The diagram on page 16 illustrates the difference between the 'comfort zone', the 'development zone' and the 'zone of fear'.

Safety officer

We strongly recommend that an appropriately qualified, responsible and experienced outdoor trainer should be appointed safety officer for every programme you run. S/he should be given powers of veto on safety matters for the whole programme. The existence of such a role and the power it possesses should be communicated to all staff and delegates.

Safety sack

We always provide at least one pre-packed safety rucksack for groups carrying out any of the following:

- caving or other underground activities;
- off-road navigation;
- cliff-face work;
- water-based activities.

The rucksack contains the following:

- first aid kit;

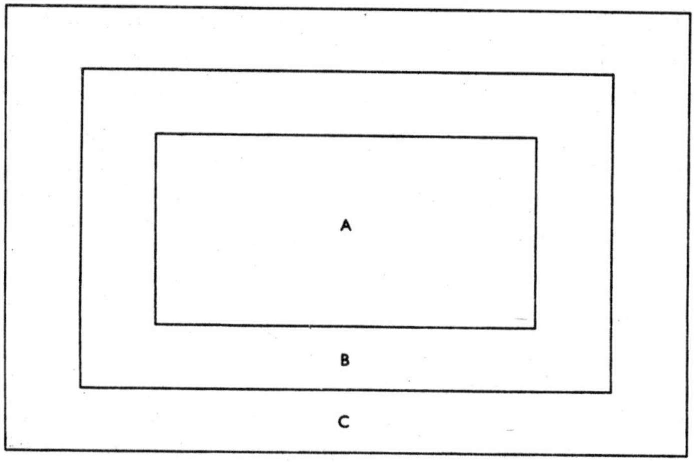

The dangers of group pressure

A = Comfort zone, the starting point for the delegate.
B = Development zone, one step from the comfort zone (therefore within the delegate's grasp).
C = Zone of fear. Pressurizing someone to enter this zone is dangerous.

- sleeping-bag;
- survival bag;
- high-energy food (chocolate, mint-cake, etc.);
- cooker and fuel in a non-leak container;
- waterproof matches and lighter;
- fresh water in a non-leak container;
- tea, coffee, dried soup.

Attitudes to safety

Safety is more than a matter of rules and regulations. Our experience is that the safest programmes are those in which all involved take a mature and balanced attitude to the tasks, have had enough preparation time to do a solid job of setting up, and know exactly what is required of them.

Trainer exhaustion leads to very real risks and should be avoided. Again, the lesson is to allow sufficient preparation time. Trainers who have spent half the night setting up exercises are not the safest of people. A penny-pinching attitude towards preparation never pays.

To summarize, only so much safety lore can be encoded. A further key to safety is able, observant and rested trainers.

CHAPTER 2

CLASSES OF EXERCISES: GENERAL INFORMATION

INTRODUCTION

In this section, we look at each class of exercises, and give some useful information on equipment, safety, and human and geographical resources.

Adapting exercises to suit your needs

We include information on variations with the facilitators' notes for each exercise. We would also urge you to experiment with variations of your own. These might be by linking exercises in a particular series, or by adding your own 'twist' to a task. It is particularly simple to do this with car park or field exercises. In doing so, consider the following:

- In what ways will the adaptation improve the 'fit' of the exercise with the group's development needs?
- How will safety be affected?
- Will additional equipment be needed?
- Ensure that exercises have more than one way of being achieved. Experience shows that 'one-solution' exercises are quite unsatisfying to delegates.

CAR PARK OR FIELD EXERCISES

Perhaps the easiest to set up, this class has become increasingly popular because the tasks can be carried out in most areas, even urban sites. Nevertheless, there are some limits:

- Nothing is more off-putting to a group than having its best efforts observed by non-participating colleagues or the general public. Make sure that the area chosen has sufficient privacy.
- Exercises take up a lot of space. For safety reasons, ensure that groups working alongside each other are sufficiently far apart not to interfere with each other.
- Grass surfaces are better than concrete ones. Scaffolding and similar equipment is much less likely to slip on a grass surface, and delegates are usually more comfortable spending a day standing on grass than on harder surfaces.

Equipment

Each exercise has its own equipment list. Finding this equipment is relatively easy, with builders' merchants, garden centres and iron-mongers providing most of the resources. We also offer the following advice:

- Scaffolding is inexpensive to hire for short periods and hardly worth buying. The well-known national stockholders are admirably efficient in delivery and collection. Do not skimp on connectors – hire about twice as many as you think you will actually need. Use alloy, not steel scaffolding.
- Stockholders tend not to hire scaffold wrenches, but they can be purchased from builders' merchants and are not expensive.
- Do not use scaffold planks – they are too weak to take people's weight if unsupported. We find that joist-standard planks are much more robust.
- If you purchase 45-gallon drums, ensure that these are new or from a reputable secondhand dealer (under 'Drums, kegs, barrels and casks' in Yellow Pages). Keep an eye on metal drums if you purchase these, as they are prone to rusting over time.
- Some large towns have rope wholesalers (under 'Rope, twine and string' in Yellow Pages). If so, purchase from these, as their prices are much better than hardware stores, or specialist sailing shops. Polypropylene rope is sufficient for most lightweight exercises, but may deteriorate with use.

Safety

Because they take place in familiar surroundings, it is easy – but wrong – to feel that these exercises have no risks attached. This is not so, and you must particularly be aware that:

- Delegates sometimes display a stunning disregard for the laws of physics when building structures. Be prepared to intervene when something obviously unsafe (you can tell by looking!) is being built.
- A rope suspended across a gap between the top of two free-standing scaffolding tripods will, when weight is put on it, cause the tripods to topple towards one another. Intervene before weight is put on the rope if groups try this obvious but unsafe method of gap-crossing. All scaffold exercises in this manual can be achieved more readily by other, safer, means.
- The key to all safety observation is to remain alert and to avoid distractions. You or your colleagues must do this on all exercises.
- We have included a detailed handout on safety matters related to scaffolding exercises. This should be given to all participants, and talked through with delegates, before such exercises.
- Personal safety equipment issued to delegates should always be of the highest standard and fit for its purpose. In particular, ensure appropriate helmets are used. In water-based activities, always use canoe helmets. Climbing helmets are dangerous in water, as they take in water. For climbing and caving activities, the helmets are usually interchangeable. For other uses, such as working with scaffolding, any industrial safety helmet will suffice, but any of the specialist helmets mentioned will serve equally well.

NAVIGATION EXERCISES

The term 'navigation exercise' often brings to mind visions of exhausted groups expeditioning for miles over wild country. The closing scenes of the film *She'll be wearing Pink Pyjamas* sum up the popular view of what navigation in the outdoors is about.

This is a shame because navigation exercises – particularly for managers – should be about such things as planning, communicating, and setting and meeting targets. Pleasant tiredness is one thing, but people doing a management exercise should not become exhausted – they generally learn little about the art of management by putting one foot in front of the other for hours on end.

The exercises in this manual all contain a major element of management planning and decision making. We have added a sample of each exercise's layout in particular locations, but it is likely that you will need to tailor them to suit the locations from which you work.

Distance covered depends on the terrain, but we suggest that for on-foot exercises the following guidelines are a useful aid to planning timing:

- for urban/road/track-based exercises without a major element of uphill walking: 5km (3 miles) per hour[1];
- for similar, but with a greater element of uphill[2] walking: 4km (2.5 miles) per hour;
- for track/footpath work in non-hilly country: 4km (2.5 miles) per hour;
- for track/footpath work in hilly country: 3km (2 miles) per hour.

These take time spent clue-searching into account, but we subscribe to the view that 'Hunt the Thimble' is not an activity for mature people, and recommend that you place clues, etc., so that they are not easily seen by members of the general public, but are relatively easy to find for delegates or others who are actually searching for them, e.g. at the foot of road signs, gateposts, etc. If you are going to *really* conceal clues, allow more time for the exercises.

Location

There is no limit to the places in which geographical exercises can be run. Our recent experiences include the melange of industrial estates, gravel pits and residential developments around Slough, the

[1] There is a popular view that 6km (4 miles) per hour is a fair speed for fit adults. Our recommendations assume that some delegates are not particularly fit.

[2] The textbooks say that walking downhill is just as difficult as walking uphill. We have found this to be true of muscular effort, but untrue as far as heart/lung stress is concerned.

flatlands of rural Essex, mountain valleys in mid-Wales and the Scottish Highlands.

The only areas which we would not recommend are those in which delegates might be at risk from lawless or violent elements. We also usually avoid areas in which navigation by compass is necessary, as such skills take time to teach, and even greater practice before delegates achieve real proficiency.

Ordnance Survey maps

These are invaluable aids to setting up exercises and are available in a very wide variety of scales. Copying them is illegal, but a licence to copy limited numbers of A5 portions of a specific map can be purchased from the Ordnance Survey (phone 0703 792000 for details) at quite reasonable rates.

We also strongly recommend the use of Silva Romer grid referencing aids and a map-wheel, a very useful device for calculating distances.

This manual includes a self-teaching map-reading guide which can also be used as input notes or handouts. This is based on the 1:25,000 *Pathfinder* and *Outdoor Leisure* series, which we find best for general use.

Pathfinder maps can be purchased at HMSO for each stationery office's region, or nationally from Northern Map Supplies (0114 2582660). Most first-world countries produce similar scale maps or acceptable 1:50,000 scale maps. These can sometimes be obtained from Northern Maps or, if the maps exist at all, Stanfords book and map shop in Long Acre, Covent Garden (0171 836 1321). The appropriate local maps are also usually readily available from stationers and post offices.

Safety

Group safety notes for navigation exercises are set out on a separate sheet. These are also for your guidance. They should be issued to all delegates taking part in navigation exercises and talked through with groups.

Access law

Access law in England and Wales is highly complex, and at the time of writing subject to a change which may make trespass a criminal rather than civil offence. Summed up, the law is as follows:

- Trespass is presumed unless you are on a public right of way.
- This applies less stringently to open land above 610m (2,000 ft) in which you can presume right of access unless specifically debarred by fences, signs, etc.
- Certain parts of England and Wales, notably the Peak District, contain large tracts of upland to which open access has been agreed. Such land is occasionally subject to the temporary withdrawal of access concessions for such sensible purposes as lambing or the presence of shooting parties. The relevant National Park Authority offices keep up-to-date details.
- Large areas of forest, coast and upland (particularly much of that owned by the National Trust and Forestry Commission) are open to access. It is best to check beforehand if you plan to use such land.
- There are many small pockets of open common land throughout Britain. Local knowledge is necessary to know where to find these.

Access law in Scotland (and most of the rest of the world) is more liberal.

Good practice

We recommend that, with the exceptions above, groups keep to recognized public rights of way, concessionary paths, or roads.

Clues and other items left for groups to discover should be put out a few hours before the exercise concerned and be unobtrusive. Any not retrieved by groups should be cleared up quickly after the exercise. To avoid misunderstandings, it is best to mark clues with a sticker stating that they are part of a training exercise and will be collected.

Outdoor skills trainers

It may be that you require the services of freelance outdoor pursuits trainers. A great many names and addresses can be obtained from the *Outdoor Source Book* published annually by Adventure Education, 39 Brunswick Square, Penrith, Cumbria CA11 7LS. Alternatively, contact us for advice via Kogan Page.

WATER-BASED EXERCISES

Although Britain is surrounded by water and has no shortage of inland resources, there are a variety of factors which limit availability:

- Coastal waters may well not be safe for lightweight vessels.
- Access to much river mileage and lake acreage is controlled by fishing clubs, whose members are not keen to see their rural retreat spoiled by loud groups of managers apparently playing on rafts or in canoes.
- Some inland water is polluted enough for no-one to wish running the risk of infection. This applies even to some apparently clear water, which may be polluted in invisible ways or infected with Weill's disease, a very serious (even life-threatening) disease carried by rats.
- Some waters may be sufficiently turbulent to represent a real risk to delegates. In coastal (and some inland) waters, turbulence and currents may not be visible.

As a consequence of the above, it is useful to have either local knowledge or contact with a local expert who will be able to advise you on safe launching points.

Water access seems to be improving in some ways. Some water authorities have undergone a real change of attitude regarding access. An example is the exemplary arrangements at Severn-Trent Water's Carsington facility, where access is not merely permitted, but encouraged.

Equipment

Each exercise has its own equipment list. As well as actual rafting equipment, canoes or kayaks and the relevant sundries such as paddles, etc., every delegate should wear an appropriate buoyancy aid. We suggest that non-swimmers and weak swimmers have a full-size government-approved life-jacket, whilst a buoyancy aid will be sufficient for strong swimmers.

Rafting equipment can be sourced from a variety of places. We find that garden centres are good for strong inexpensive spars (we use 8ft ones), and 45-gallon drums are best bought new or from reputable secondhand dealers.

In addition, an adequate safety boat should be provided and used. It is a good idea to supplement this with a throw-line or similar which can be used from the shore.

Building rafts

There are many ways for groups to build rafts which do the job effectively. We never give much detailed instruction on design, as this takes the initiative away from the group. However, we often give instruction in tying clove hitches, bowlines, and making square and diagonal lashings. Such instruction is beyond the scope of this manual, but we recommend a variety of publications from the Scout Association.

We also offer a few useful tips. These are as follows:

- Place the barrels, the source of buoyancy, at the farthest sensible extremities of the raft, as this makes for greater stability.
- Ensure that the barrels are extremely well secured to the frame of the raft.

Safety

Water-based activities have potential for danger, which may be considerably reduced by operating to responsible safety standards. These include ensuring that properly qualified staff (see pages 41–43) are present in a ratio of 1:6. We have provided detailed group safety notes which should be issued to all groups taking part in water-based activities, and to which you should adhere.

CLIFF-FACE EXERCISES

Britain has a number of areas in which the cliff-face exercises in this manual can be run. Principal inland areas include Dartmoor and South Devon, much of Wales, the Wye Valley, the Peak District, the Lake District, North Yorkshire, Northumbria, and much of the Scottish borders, Highlands and Islands. Areas we have also used include the Mendips, the Forest of Dean, Leicestershire and Kent, although access to the highly erodible sandstone of the latter area is limited for reasons of conservation.

We have only used coastal cliffs in the Aberdovey area, but it may be that other sea-cliffs are suitable.

Many of the above areas have climbing guides in print which give invaluable information as to likely sites and access requirements, but pre-course visits are indispensable, as a good climbing venue may not be terribly useful for such exercises as 'Haul of Fame'. Some of the larger areas have crags which are openly acknowledged as good for beginners.

A local instructor (there are many good freelance outdoor people available) will be an invaluable help to you in pinpointing suitable locations.

Adapting exercises to meet your needs

The climbing exercises in this manual are fairly specific and do not lend themselves easily to adaptation except in terms of numbers participating. The exercises requiring multi-group performance can all be adapted for single-group working, and vice versa. They should also provide an impetus for you to design your own exercises.

Equipment

Climbing equipment is expensive and requires some maintenance. It is therefore better to leave provision of equipment to qualified safety staff, unless you are a keen climber or intend to use cliff faces very frequently.

Safety

Cliff-face exercises have potential for physical and psychological danger. This is considerably reduced by operating to responsible safety standards.

We have provided detailed group safety notes which should be issued to all groups taking part in crag activities, and to which you should adhere.

UNDERGROUND EXERCISES

The interaction of water and limestone has given Britain many natural caves. In addition, humanity has been extracting minerals from the ground for thousands of years.

As a result, much of Britain has access to some kind of underground location, natural or artificial. Exploration of these has been going on in a steady and organized way for over a century, and there are hundreds of caving clubs and mines historical societies active in this country, as well as many more non-affiliated cavers.

Areas of Britain with large numbers of significant natural caves include North Yorkshire, Derbyshire, South Wales and the Mendips. Other areas with smaller concentrations include South Devon, the Gower peninsula, Pembrokeshire, East Clwyd, the Lake District and small corners of the Scottish Highlands and Islands.

Most of the above areas have up-to-date caving guides in print. These guides are an invaluable aid, giving detailed locations, grade of difficulty, equipment required, hazards, access requirements, and so on.

The larger areas have caves which are suitable for novices and to which access is simple. Local cave leaders will know which these are.

In Britain, metal mining areas include Sussex, Cornwall, Devon, much of Wales, the Peak District, the Mendips, parts of the Lake District, Yorkshire, the Northeast, parts of Leicestershire, the Forest of Dean, the Scottish Southern Uplands, and the Isle of Man. If the brief is broadened to include other minerals, more of Wales and parts of Wiltshire are added. Abandoned coal mines should be avoided at all costs due to the extreme danger associated with them.

Although there is an apparent wealth of underground locations available, a variety of visible and invisible hazards reduce the total which can be used by groups. Radon gas, a carcinogen, is present in a number of caves. Mines may have particular hazards such as hidden shafts which make them too dangerous to enter, and both caves and mines are occasionally subject to high levels of carbon dioxide which can be life-threatening through oxygen deprivation.

Adapting exercises to suit your needs

The underground exercises in this manual can be adapted and extended to meet a real variety of training needs. For example, exercise 'Mine of Information' can be widened and extended into a multi-day project-management exercise with video-presentations, interviews with old miners, examination of the way the mine influenced local life, and so on. This has resulted in a very effective and worthwhile exercise.

Equipment

Each exercise has its own equipment list. Miners' lamps and so on demand heavy and constant maintenance to remain efficient, and unless you are a keen underground explorer it is rarely worth purchasing them. They can usually be supplied by skills trainers or hired from caving shops.

Basic surveying equipment (which can also be used in above-ground survey exercises) is not expensive and can be bought from hardware stores, outdoor shops and educational suppliers. The simple clinometers provided by the latter are perfectly good for the levels of accuracy required.

Safety

Underground exercises have potential for physical and psychological danger, which is considerably reduced by operating to responsible safety standards. These include ensuring that properly qualified staff are present in a ratio of 1:4.

We have provided detailed groups safety notes which should be issued to all groups taking part in underground activities, and to which you should adhere.

CHAPTER 3

THE THEORETICAL BASIS

INTRODUCTION

The aim of this chapter is to explain some of the advantages and disadvantages of Management Development Outdoors, and examine some of the fundamentals of a successful programme. As purchasers of this book will possibly never read this part we kept it short, but if the reader would like to learn more we suggest the book *Management Development Outdoors, A practical guide to getting the best results* by the same authors and publisher.

The outdoors provides an extremely powerful medium for training managers in new skills or helping them to improve old ones. This is largely because outdoor learning is experiential in nature. It therefore makes sense to spend some time examining experiential theory and its application in the outdoors:

EXPERIENTIAL LEARNING

Experiential learning is a training method that moves away from the theoretical and parrot-fashion learning methods of traditionalist education.

When thinking about learning, most of us think about school, teachers and textbooks. In most schools learning was a process by which the teacher taught and had the responsibility for pupils' success or otherwise, usually measured by tests and examinations. The student was there to absorb, memorize and repeat information as necessary.

Unfortunately, most management training is the same. Flip-charts have replaced chalk-boards, handouts have largely replaced textbooks, classrooms are called training rooms. Handouts and textbooks are essentially concerned with abstract ideas and concepts, and there is a continued, if not growing, emphasis on academic qualifications during recruitment.

The result of the above is that training is often viewed as:

- a special activity divorced from the real world;
- only concerned with abstract concepts;
- possessing a predictable temporal end point.

Consequently learning is seen as a separate activity, largely irrelevant to our working lives, but this is ineffective in a world where accelerating change is one of the few constants. We now live in that world, with career and job changes occurring at an ever-accelerating rate. The ability to learn is itself among the most important skills that we can develop.

Experiential training has evolved to challenge these assumptions, and provide more effective means for people to continue to learn and develop throughout life.

We all learn from experience. By burning ourselves we learn to avoid heated objects, by testing our parents' (or bosses!) patience we learn about acceptable standards of behaviour and the consequences of transgressing. Every day we have experiences from which we learn; education has even been defined as changes in behaviour caused by experience.

Some things simply cannot be learned from books or lectures. Examples range from riding a bicycle to falling in love. So experiential learning is a natural and constant life process on which all development training, particularly Management Development Outdoors aims to capitalize.

Experiential learning can be seen as a four-stage cycle:

1. concrete, personal experiences followed by:
2. observation of and reflection upon one's experiences, which leads to:
3. the formation of generalizations and abstract concepts, leading to:
4. hypotheses to be tested by future actions, which in turn lead to new experiences.

A number of important things need to be remembered about this cycle:

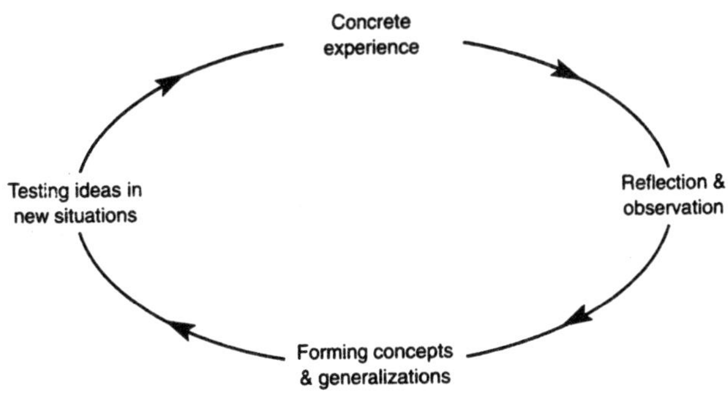

The experiential learning cycle

- *The cycle is continuously recurring.* We constantly test the implications of what we have learned and modify our concepts as a consequence of what we see happening in each new situation. Much learning is indeed relearning, especially on a Management Development programme, but this is still important and valuable, if only by bringing old learning back into focus to confirm the reasons behind good habits and challenge those behind bad or outdated behaviours.
- *The objectives we set ourselves govern the direction of our learning.* We look for and interpret experiences, according to our needs and goals as we perceive them. Unclear goals lead to haphazard and ineffective learning. For this reason alone the success and failure of many programmes is directly attributable to the quality of objective-setting.
- *We all have personal preferences.* How we learn and which part of the cycle is most meaningful to us depends on who we are. It should be noted that overemphasis on one or more of the elements in the learning process can lead to ineffective and incomplete learning. Experience without reflection does not help learning; we would repeat experiences, rather like the rat which cannot find its way out of a maze because it keeps forgetting the results of its earlier attempts. Similarly, theory without the opportunity to experiment is limiting and sometimes justifies the oft-repeated blue-collar jibes about college boys.

This should be carefully considered when designing any training event, but particularly an MDO programme. All elements of the cycle should be adequately covered and facilitated.

David A. Kolb's *Learning Style Inventory* examines these preferences in some detail and can be a useful inclusion in a programme.[1]

Experiential learning is based on three assumptions and provides further clues to the design of a successful programme:

- People learn best when personally involved in the learning experience;
- Knowledge, to be truly meaningful, has to be discovered by the individual;
- People are more committed to learning when they are free to identify and pursue their own goals.

Experiential learning therefore places the emphasis on:

- direct, personal experience;
- building individuals' commitment to development;
- giving learners as great a responsibility as possible for drawing conclusions.

In experiential training the responsibility for learning lies with the trainee, who therefore needs to be active and assertive in the learning role, whilst trainers should limit their role to providing effective design, and a focus for reflection and the drawing of conclusions by the trainee.

For example if delegates wished to learn about leadership they could take part in a programme designed to focus on that issue, reflecting on seen and experienced behaviour to decide for themselves what were the important lessons learnt and how best to apply them in the future.

In a well-designed experiential learning programme people will be encouraged to experiment, try new behaviours and draw their own conclusions. Theories appropriate to the situation may then be presented to help them develop frameworks to fit their own unique requirements and environment.

The motivation to learn

What motivates people to learn? Some see learning as worthwhile and enjoyable in its own right; others need extra motivation.

[1] Kolb, David A., *The Learning Style Inventory*, McBer and Co., Boston, 1976.

Obviously it is different for everyone, but experiential learning stresses a sense of success and accomplishment in learning. Motivation is based on the desirability of the goals and the chosen methods of reaching them. Kurt Lewin[1] identified four factors which lead to psychological success in learning:

- Learners are able to define their own goals.
- Goals are related to the learners' central needs and values.
- Learners are able to define the paths to accomplishing their goals.
- Goals represent a realistic level of aspiration for the learners – neither too high nor too low, but high enough to challenge and test their capabilities.

Feelings of success will only be fully realized when learners are encouraged to take as much responsibility as possible for their own behaviour. Many well-intentioned outdoor programmes fail because sessions are so tightly controlled that delegates feel more like passengers than active participants with jobs to do. Learners must at least have influence on, and preferably should control, the learning process. This can be particularly difficult when an organization tightly defines a programme's objectives. Programme designers and facilitators must carefully clarify and rationalize contracts with delegates and sponsoring organizations.

Intrinsic motivation can be enhanced by other factors. The involvement of other learners in the process is often crucial to breaking barriers, as is their approval, support and feedback – all can facilitate learning and increase the desire to learn.

Despite the criticism of some formal training methods, theory still has its place in experiential learning. Delegates often place greater confidence in their own learning when they discover that formal input supports it and appropriate models can aid understanding and retention. There is little room for the set lesson in experiential training. There is, however, much to be said for inputting theory that supports the delegates' own findings.

MDO – THE ADVANTAGES

MDO shares, but often increases, the benefits of experiential training.

---

[1] Lewin, K., *A Dynamic Theory of Personality*, McGraw Hill, New York, 1935.

Indeed, many 'outdoor' exercises can be run indoors, given enough space and imagination. It is a sad fact that to some, 'outdoors' means mountain ranges and untamed moorland. We have found that a car park, hotel garden or even city park can be perfectly adequate places to run outdoor activities.

Reality

Indoor experiential learning is often built around role-playing or business simulations, with participants acting within some situation. This can be done in outdoor exercises, but need not be, as it is easier in the outdoors to set real problems with real consequences and real constraints.

A team building a raft suffers a very real penalty if they do it badly. In effect the task, although unusual, is real. Such a task encourages and produces interpersonal processes and behaviour typical of the way the team operates. Participants are dealing with real people in genuine situations, and therefore find themselves dealing with real issues. If someone feels underused or not appreciated, it is real and often corresponds to behaviour in the workplace. The difference is that on a course, observation and review of such processes can be facilitated.

Some would argue that outdoor exercises should contain elements of role-play or imagination because this adds colour and enhances memorability, but it is not essential. Indeed, it can easily be overdone at the expense of reality.

We have seen over-enthusiastic delegates harassing innocent members of the public because of a too colourful brief. With common sense a balance can be found. We have found that telling a group they cannot touch the ground is as effective as telling them it is a mine-field. If tempted to use such devices, consider why and for whose benefit, will it enhance the learning? It is not always wrong, but sometimes superfluous and counter-productive.

Memorability

Any programme or exercise conducted in the outdoors has huge potential for strong memories: of the experience; the environment;

the weather; the learning. This is important. Anything that can assist the notoriously fallible human memory is immensely valuable to the trainer. In Management Development Outdoors, recall of events facilitates recall of learning.

There are potentially more opportunities for memorable events in the outdoors than in any other area of management development. This is especially so if the exercises include such high-profile outdoor activities as abseiling or cave-exploration, although even simple activities in the company car park contain the potential for long-term recall.

Reduced barriers to learning

To most managers the outdoors is an unusual environment. Very few have outdoor skills; even those, such as ex-soldiers, who have some skills, should find they are of only limited value on a well-designed outdoor programme. So essentially all participants start off on an equal footing.

Because seniority and expertise at the workplace are neutralized, behaviourial skills and process awareness become more important. Everyone has something to learn and the outdoors gives them the opportunity to do so.

Even physical fitness should not be a problem. Properly designed exercises should have elements in them which allow everyone to contribute, regardless of health, age or fitness. We have seen unfit and disabled people attend outdoor programmes, contribute fully, learn and help others to learn.

Shared experience

Because the outdoor experience is so unusual and absorbing, many delegates – even from disparate backgrounds – build very close bonds of companionship which far outlast the course itself.

If the delegates are from the same company or workplace, the bond will be even stronger and more likely to continue. Early reinforcement of the bonding mechanism by regular and relevant follow-up greatly enhances the process.

This is one reason why outdoor programmes are so popular for team-building. It helps people to appreciate each other more, and to understand the value of diversity in teams. If the shared experiences are very memorable, the bonding process can be continually reinforced by recalling the activity, and also by identifying similar situations at work – 'This is just like when we . . .'

People will not always return from a programme loving each other. They may simply understand each other better. We remember a salesman who commented after a programme that he still didn't like his production manager, but now understood him better and felt he could work with him. This was borne out in their future working relationship which, although never close, was more cordial and much more productive.

DISADVANTAGES OF MDO

These are few and not insuperable, but important enough to mention, and understanding them will help you to avoid them.

Too enjoyable

It is quite possible that participants become so wrapped up in enjoying an outdoor exercise that learning is lost. This can largely be overcome by careful facilitation of the review process, helping delegates to recognize the power of the experience as well as the enjoyment.

We sometimes find that teams who overemphasize the enjoyment factor tend also to have problems taking each other seriously at work. The facilitator's role with such teams is to ensure that the learning – which may be painful – is not avoided.

Role adoption

Some people may overreact to the 'colour' of an exercise and, as in the example mentioned earlier, behave abnormally. This has an obviously detrimental effect on the learning process but can be avoided by careful exercise design – and we have found that an exercise is just as valid when played straight as when a spurious storyline is incorporated – and overcome by careful review and feedback.

Denial

Delegates sometimes complain that the exercises are not realistic or are an unfair reflection of their working environment. There are two reasons for this:

- It is reasonable criticism. If so, efforts should be made to remedy the situation. It is unhelpful and potentially destructive to learning to ask someone from a particular culture to behave in a way not acceptable in that culture. It would be unhelpful to encourage too much creativity and initiative in delegates from a highly structured and systemized organization.
- It is a way of avoiding real issues. Sometimes people use denial ('I wouldn't act like that in real life!') to evade unwelcome truths. This can only be dealt with by careful review.

THE EFFECTIVE OUTDOOR APPROACH

To summarize, the way to get the best out of MDO is to remember all the points we have considered, maximizing the benefits and minimizing the disadvantages. In particular, ensure that providers understand and use the principles and ethics of experiential learning.

Providers should also be able to design and deliver programmes that address the full learning cycle, taking account of individual learning styles, including:

- exercises which are full of relevant process-experience;
- review of the processes underlying the exercises to articulate the learning that took place;
- input to help delegates to make sense of their learning and put it into a legitimate framework;
- giving delegates the opportunity to plan how they will use the new ideas in future situations, initially in the next exercise, but also on return to work.

LEVELS OF PHYSICALITY

It is commonly believed that all MDO programmes are highly physical and demanding. Some are, including some very good ones. However, if this medium is as powerful as we believe it to be, it should be as universally accessible as possible. Therefore the best programmes will have roles and opportunities for the manager who is overweight, disabled, of a weak disposition or just afraid of heights. These conditions, after all, do not usually prevent them performing in the workplace, so should not on the programme, which is intended to be, at least in part, a metaphor for work.

If you know your delegates it is easier to design to suit them, but if not, prepare roles for all types of people. It can be limiting if the programme is not demanding enough but, for quality learning, too physical is the greater danger. Have roles which require the super-fit salesman or squash champion accountant to run up a hill, but balance this with a recording or coordinating role for the older, sport-hating personnel manager.

Forced marches across the wild country, ascents of mountains and wild-water rafting expeditions may help to form close emotional bonds with fellow-delegates, but may also foster inappropriate elitism, unproductive divisions and even intolerance.

Uses for which Management Development Outdoors has been shown to be effective include:

- leadership training;
- project management;
- team development;
- improving communications;
- encouraging creativity;
- stress management;
- interpersonal skills;
- change management;
- planning;
- decision-making;
- risk management.

CHAPTER 4

SAFETY PROCEDURES

INTRODUCTION

Safety has to be the overriding concern in all practical exercises. This is particularly true in the outdoors, where the potential for danger is often higher. Even when the tasks are relatively innocuous, there is always some risk. People can do or attempt strange things under the pressure of an outdoor learning event. We believe it is good safety practice to expect and insure against all hazards, no matter how bizarre or insignificant.

You may therefore find some of our safety guidelines pedantic or petty. We make no apologies for this, rather we would point to our successful safety record. In the final analysis Management Development Outdoors is a medium for management development, not for generating danger, fear or excitement.

There are some specific safety guidelines on the following pages for water activities, climbing exercises, underground activities, walking and when using scaffolding. We recommend that these pages are regularly reviewed by all staff involved and copies issued to delegates. However, even these notes are not exhaustive. Some safety aspects require specialized staff, as detailed below, and no guidelines could replace their input.

GENERAL

Safety staff

For many of the exercises described in this book it is reasonable to combine the safety role with facilitating the learning. For some, however, the two roles may need to be separated. This is particularly true of climbing, caving and water activities. If you do not have relevant skills, it is imperative that you hire people with them. The minimum specialist qualifications recommended and some sources of appropriately qualified people are included under the appropriate headings.

First aid

This is a particularly important aspect of safety and should not be neglected. Appropriate first aid kits should be available at all times and staff should be properly qualified to use them. If you are planning any work in wild country, at least one staff member should be a qualified Mountain First Aider. However, for most work First Aid at Work is an appropriate qualification. Courses to obtain these qualifications are run under the auspices of the Red Cross, St. John's Ambulance and St. Andrew's Ambulance.

SAFETY IN WATER-BASED EXERCISES

Safety instructions

Groups should be told or reminded of the appropriate guidelines, outlined below, before any task in or on water.

If Canadian canoes or kayaks are to be used, prior instruction by properly qualified trainers (BCU or its overseas equivalent) is essential.

Safety boats

Safety boats should be on the water at all times that rafts, boats, canoes or kayaks are being launched or sailed. For preference, at least one should be powered by an engine, but stable rowing boats are an acceptable substitute on still water.

Safety equipment

Canoeing helmets and buoyancy aids (for strong swimmers) or full life-jackets (for weak swimmers) are a must. Ensure that waist-belts are secured on these, as otherwise there is a risk of the wearer and the aid becoming separated. Most outdoor trainers possess these items, which should be checked for continued buoyancy on a regular basis, as they are subject to deterioration with continued use.

Have a full safety sack available, containing:

- ☐ some large towels;
- ☐ survival bag;
- ☐ water;
- ☐ energy food;
- ☐ sleeping-bag;
- ☐ stove;
- ☐ first aid kit;
- ☐ hot beverage kit.

Instruct the group to bring a change of dry clothes with them. They must wear plimsolls or trainers on their feet, as these are light. Boots, especially wellingtons, can fill with water and cause people to be pulled under.

Bring a large flask of tea or coffee. *On no account* should you lace this with alcohol, as, although this may make people feel good, it reduces their body temperature.

Someone with a throwing line on the bank is very useful backup to the safety boats. Such lines are available from outdoor shops.

Rafting

Any raft built should be checked before launching by safety staff to assess its water-worthiness. Safety staff should have the power to veto the launch of any vessel built, on grounds of safety. In doing so, they should act like the Health and Safety Inspectorate, offering advice as well as criticism.

Rafts should only be launched by being taken to the water and being gently lowered whilst remaining level. There is real danger if the group hauls the raft into a vertical position and then lowers it into the water like a jib. See diagram below.

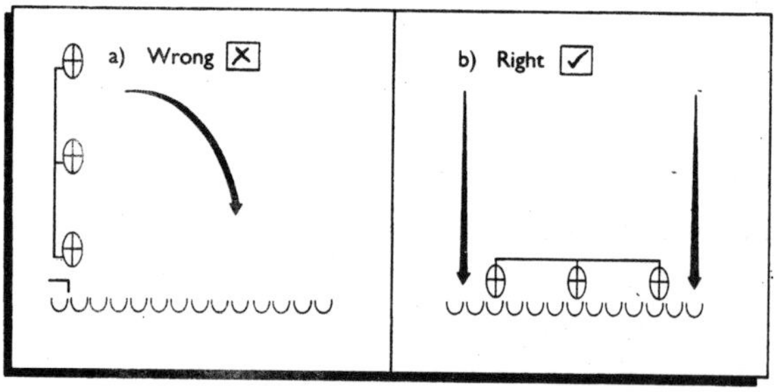

Launching a raft: a) wrong; b) right

Be sure you know the provenance of any 25- or 45-gallon drums used. These are best when bought new or from a responsible secondhand dealer who will have 'reamed' the inside very fully.

Safety staff

Safety staff in the correct ratio of 1:6 should supervise all water activities. If delegates are on the water an appropriate safety boat should be on the water at all times. For preference, at least one should be powered by an engine.

GROUP NOTES

Safety in water-based exercises

- If your exercise requires rafts to be built, these should be checked by safety staff before launching to assess water-worthiness. Safety staff have the power to veto the launch of any vessel built, on grounds of safety. In doing so, they will act like the Health and Safety Inspectorate, offering advice as well as criticism.
- Safety boats should be on the water at all times that rafts, boats, canoes or kayaks are being launched or sailed.
- Canoeing helmets and buoyancy aids (for strong swimmers) or full life-jackets (for weak swimmers) are a must. Ensure that waist-belts are secured on these, as otherwise there is a risk of the wearer and the aid becoming separated.
- A full safety sack is available, together with some large towels.
- Bring a change of dry clothes with you. You should also wear plimsolls or trainers on your feet, as these are light.
- A large flask of tea or coffee is available at all times when people are on or near the water. This is for emergency use only.
- Rafts should only be launched by being taken to the water and being gently lowered whilst remaining level. There is real danger if you haul the raft into a vertical position and then lower it into the water like a jib.
- If Canadian canoes or kayaks are to be used, all people using them must have received instruction and authorization from BCU (or its overseas equivalent) qualified trainers.
- Canoeing helmets should be worn by all involved in the construction or sailing of rafts at all times that these activities are taking place.
- Staff may need to add further safety rules depending on conditions at the time.

SAFETY IN CLIFF-FACE EXERCISES

Safety instructions

Groups should be told or reminded of the appropriate guidelines, outlined below, prior to any task involving climbing or similar activities on rock-faces.

Safety equipment

Equipment for these exercises should be of the highest quality and standard of maintenance. Advice on appropriate equipment, and often the equipment itself, can be provided by hired safety staff. This should include:

- ☐ safety ropes;
- ☐ abseil ropes;
- ☐ harnesses;
- ☐ climbing helmets;
- ☐ other climbing hardware;
- ☐ rigging ropes;
- ☐ hauling ropes;
- ☐ belts;
- ☐ gloves.

Safety staff

Technical/safety staff should be properly qualified. The current minimum qualification is the Single Pitch Supervisor's award. In addition to this, you must satisfy yourself that you are happy with the way the relevant trainers conduct themselves. These staff must have complete powers in the area of safety, including power to overrule decisions made by process tutors.

A ratio of one safety staff member to every four delegates is recommended.

Prior training for groups can be provided by the above, and can vary from none at all (but with group access to written notes on the relevant climbing technology) right through to every delegate having abseiled under the control of a safety tutor. We usually opt for a middle course where some have received hands-on training in hauling, some in abseiling, and others in safety-rope procedures. Typically, this will have been in a less-than-real situation, perhaps a hotel garden or group room. The advantage of this approach is that the groups as a whole has all the necessary knowledge, but no one individual is an 'expert'. This, combined with the reality of the situation, encourages a healthy sharing of knowledge.

Psychological safety

No member of staff or delegate should apply undue pressure on delegates who do not wish to climb, abseil, be hauled, or operate the safety rope. Staff should tactfully intervene with delegates putting such pressure on others.

An example of a less threatening role within a climbing exercise is the job of hauling, which should take place well away from the edge of the cliff, and therefore provides 'non-cliff' people with a necessary task to perform.

Staff should ensure that non-cliff people still feel part of the group after the exercise.

GROUP NOTES

Safety in cliff face-exercises

- Technical/safety staff have complete powers in the area of safety.
- All karabiners must be safely secured.
- No group member may go closer than 2 metres from the edge of the cliff unless correctly roped-up.
- No stepping on ropes, even when ropes are not in use (minute particles of grit can penetrate the outer mantle of the rope and damage the core).
- No smoking near ropes at any time, even when ropes are coiled and not in use. (Ash can damage rope in the same way as grit.)
- Correctly fastened helmets and belts will be worn at all times, and gloves when indicated by staff.
- Group members may not proceed over the edge or up from the bottom of the cliff without prior checking by a member of safety staff.
- Group members should not put others under undue pressure to perform any of the cliff-face tasks.
- Other safety conditions may need to be applied depending on conditions at the time.

GROUP NOTES

Safety when working with scaffolding

- Ensure that any structure built is sound, with all scaffold couplers firmly secured by spanner/wrench. Ensure also that tripods, if built, will not 'kick' when leverage is applied to them.
- If any hard object such as a coupler or spanner/wrench is to be thrown between areas, ensure that all present are aware of this, and that the items are not thrown in anyone's direction.
- Take care when lifting to ensure that you do not take on too much weight, and that you *bend your legs, not your back*.
- If you suffer with back problems, leave the lifting to others.
- Carry longer scaffold poles either with one person at each end (like a stretcher) or by dragging them with one end on the ground, like a Native American travois.
- Do not attempt to catch hard objects.
- Ensure that all present are wearing helmets and gloves at all times.
- Take real care if climbing on scaffold structures. You may need to enlist the help of others in this.
- Do not climb on unstable structures.
- Ensure that any flexible scaffold couplings used do not run the risk of rotating unexpectedly – if someone has an arm between the poles thus joined, severe bruising can occur.
- Take special care after the exercise has finished and when dismantling any structures – always ensure that all poles are being securely held, thus minimizing the risk of unplanned structural collapse.
- *Organize* dismantling – it's too easy to relax after the task has been completed, and this is dangerous.

SAFETY IN NAVIGATION EXERCISES

Group safety notes for geographical exercises are set out on a separate sheet. These are also for your guidance, and should be issued to all delegates taking part in geographical exercises and talked through with groups. In addition:

- Issue each sub-group with a whistle for *emergency use only.*
- If any distance over 1km is to be travelled off road, they should be accompanied by a qualified staff member and carry a full safety sack, containing:

  - ☐ Sleeping bag
  - ☐ Stove
  - ☐ First aid kit
  - ☐ Hot beverage kit
  - ☐ Survival bag
  - ☐ Water
  - ☐ Energy food

- Beware of the level of physical stress to which groups can subject themselves, and do not allow them to be split into sub-groups of less than 3. This means that if one group member has a mishap, there is someone to stay with him/her and someone else to fetch help. Although our experience over 10 years is accident-free, it is worth remembering that people can twist ankles in urban and lowland environments as well as in wild country.
- Delegates with heart or lung problems, or a history of these, should only participate in the planning phases of serious on-foot exercises. To overcome isolation, we usually give them an observing role after the planning phase, and they accompany the patrolling vehicle(s) and observe the groups whenever possible. The feedback they give is often very useful.
- People can dehydrate easily. Provide drinks for them to carry in their rucksacks. *Do not* under any circumstances provide alcohol – this exacerbates the problem.
- During the active phase of the exercise, patrol the routes and keep tabs on each sub-group. If you have sufficient staff, have one staff-member accompany each group.

GROUP NOTES

Safety in navigation exercises

- On no account should you drive vehicles. Some geographical exercises provide for staff to transport you. The task brief will give details if this is the case. In all other cases, walk.
- Before you leave the start-point, inform staff of your planned destinations and your estimated times of arrival.
- If walking on roads, you should walk in single file, facing oncoming traffic, except on 'blind' bends.
- Depending on terrain, gradients, etc., this exercise may be unsuitable for people with heart or lung illnesses. If in doubt, consult staff.
- Clothing depends on the prevailing conditions. If any 'off-road' work at all is involved, you should wear walking boots. Do not wear waterproofs on hot days (especially dry ones), but carry them with you.
- *Do not* under any circumstances consume alcohol during the exercise – this dehydrates people. We have provided refreshing drinks for you to carry.
- You should not split into groups of less than 3 for off-road exercises or groups of 2 on-road. You should remain in sight and sound of each other at all times. This is in order that if one group member has a mishap, there is someone to stay with them and someone else to fetch help.
- In the case of a mishap off-road, one team member should stay with the injured delegate, whilst another returns to the nearest point of vehicular access. The delegate staying with the injured person should blow a whistle for 6 consecutive one-second blasts, followed by one minute's silence. This is the only use to which whistles should be put.
- If travelling more than one kilometre off the road, you will be accompanied by a qualified staff member and must carry a safety sack as provided.

SAFETY IN UNDERGROUND EXERCISES

Safety instructions

Underground exercises have potential for physical and psychological danger. Such potential is considerably reduced by operating to responsible safety standards. We have provided detailed group safety notes which should be issued to all groups taking part in underground activities, and to which you should adhere.

Caves and mines with pitches (areas requiring ropework), ducks and sumps (areas where the cave roof dips to below surface water-level), or active streamways liable to flooding *must* be avoided, as must underground locations liable to roof falls. There are semi-acknowledged 'beginners' caves and mines in many areas, and it is wise to stick to these. Mines should be of the 'adit' type requiring walking or crawling entry.

Some areas of Britain contain underground locations in which high concentrations of radon gas (a carcinogen) exist. Centres in these areas operate a voluntary ban on underground exploration, and you should honour this.

Undue social pressure should never be put on delegates who do not wish to go underground. Staff should tactfully intervene with delegates putting such pressure on others. Useful roles should be provided for those who do not wish to go underground and their contribution should be acknowledged at the end of the exercise.

Safety equipment

Delegates should be provided with suitable clothing for going underground, such as boilersuits and wellington boots. They should also have a reliable light source. Miners' lamps and so on demand heavy and constant maintenance to remain efficient, and unless you are a keen underground explorer it is rarely worth purchasing them. They can usually be supplied by skills trainers or hired from caving shops. Each group should be provided with a portable, watertight container inside which is:

- ☐ first aid kit;
- ☐ energy food;

- ☐ survival bag;
- ☐ spare lights.

Equipment should be properly worn and used. Technical instructors should give instruction on this before anyone goes underground.

Safety staff

Ensure that properly qualified staff are present in a ratio of 1:4. The current appropriate technical qualification for caving staff is the Local Cave Leader's Award for the relevant area. In addition, you must satisfy yourself that you are happy with the way the trainers conduct themselves.

In some areas the Local Cave Leader's Award may suffice for leadership in mines, but in others a similar mine leadership qualification may be required. This is for two reasons:

- Safety issues in mines are somewhat different to those in caves.
- Disused mines, even if abandoned for hundreds of years, are still subject to the provisions of mine and quarry legislation. An agreement exists that these provisions (which would be prohibitively expensive to apply to abandoned mines) are modified for bona fide caving and educational groups, provided they are led by qualified people.

Properly qualified local skills trainers know the hazards of their area and are able to advise on suitable locations.

Safety staff must also have the power to overrule decisions made by process tutors on technical matters.

GROUP NOTES

Safety in caves

- Safety staff should at all times accompany those going underground in a ratio of 1:4 (or better). Safety staff have complete powers on all safety related matters, and may not be ignored.
- Equipment should be properly worn and used at all times. Safety staff will give instruction on this before anyone goes underground.
- No one should apply undue pressure to delegates who do not wish to go underground.
- You must stay within sight and sound of a member of safety staff at all times.
- You will not be permitted to negotiate pitches, ducks, sumps, or work in a cave with an active streamway liable to flooding.
- Depending on conditions, additional safety rules may be added.

GROUP NOTES

Safety in mines

- Safety staff should accompany underground groups at all times in a ratio of 1:4 or better. Safety staff have complete powers on all safety-related matters, and may not be ignored.
- The mine is of the 'adit' type requiring walking or crawling entry. You will not be required to negotiate pitches (areas requiring ropework), ducks, or sumps (areas where the mine roof dips to below surface water-level).
- Equipment should be properly worn and used. Technical instructors will give instruction on this before anyone goes underground.
- No one should apply undue social pressure to delegates who do not wish to go underground.
- You must stay within sight and sound of a member of safety staff at all times when underground.
- Depending on conditions at the time, additional safety rules may be applied.

CHAPTER 5

How to use this sourcebook

THE INDEX

We have presented the index in a matrix format. By reading down the left-hand column readers will be able to identify the development needs they wish to address. By then reading across the matrix, they will be able to identify suitable exercises.

THE EXERCISES

Each exercise has two sets of notes. The facilitator's notes give a brief introduction, numbers that can participate, an indication of the time required, the materials needed, and notes on setting up and running the exercise. There are also some suggested alternatives and variations. The group notes contain the exercise brief and should be issued to the group.

THE BACKGROUND NOTES

A series of notes on useful background theory are included at the back of the sourcebook. These are intended to provide in a concise form some conceptual frameworks which should aid learning from the exercises. They may be used as handout material, or as a source of ideas for facilitators on how to structure reviews.

Index

Exercise No.	1	2	3	4	5	6	7	8	9	10	11	12	13	14	15	16
Managing change																
Communication	■	■	■		■	■	■	■	■	■	■	■	■	■	■	■
Controlling					■		■		■		■	■	■			■
Coordinating			■	■	■	■	■		■		■	■	■	■	■	■
Creativity						■	■		■	■	■					
Decision-making	■	■						■	■					■	■	■
Delegation						■							■			
Group dynamics	■	■	■	■	■	■		■	■	■	■	■	■	■	■	■
Interpersonal skills	■	■	■		■	■	■	■	■	■	■	■	■	■	■	■
Leadership	■	■			■	■		■	■	■	■	■	■	■	■	■
Teamwork	■	■	■	■	■	■	■	■	■	■	■	■	■	■	■	■
Team-building	■	■				■		■	■	■	■	■	■	■	■	■
Listening	■	■	■		■	■	■	■	■			■	■			■
Negotiating															■	
Planning	■							■	■	■	■		■	■	■	■
Problem-solving	■	■				■	■	■	■	■	■	■	■	■	■	■
Time management														■	■	■

Exercise No.	17	18	19	20	21	22	23	24	25	26	27	28	29	30	31	32
Managing change																
Communication	■	■	■	■	■	■	■	■	■	■	■	■	■	■	■	■
Controlling				■		■		■	■	■	■		■			
Coordinating	■		■		■	■	■		■	■	■	■	■		■	■
Creativity													■			
Decision-making						■	■				■		■	■	■	■
Delegation				■	■	■		■	■	■			■			
Group dynamics	■	■	■		■	■	■	■	■	■	■	■	■	■	■	■
Interpersonal skills	■	■	■		■	■	■	■	■	■	■	■	■	■	■	■
Leadership	■	■	■	■	■	■	■	■	■	■	■	■	■	■	■	■
Teamwork	■	■	■		■	■	■	■	■	■	■	■	■	■	■	■
Team-building	■	■	■		■	■	■	■	■	■	■	■	■	■	■	■
Listening				■							■		■			
Negotiating					■		■					■	■		■	
Planning				■	■	■	■	■	■	■	■	■	■	■	■	■
Problem-solving	■	■	■	■			■				■	■	■	■	■	
Time management					■	■		■	■	■	■	■	■		■	■

Exercise No.	33	34	35	36	37	38	39	40	41	42	43	44	45	46	47	48
Managing change				■							■		■	■	■	■
Communication	■	■	■	■	■	■	■	■	■	■	■	■	■	■	■	■
Controlling		■	■	■				■		■	■		■	■	■	■
Coordinating	■	■		■	■	■	■		■	■	■	■	■	■	■	■
Creativity		■	■	■				■							■	■
Decision-making	■	■		■		■	■		■	■	■	■	■	■	■	■
Delegation	■			■		■		■	■	■	■	■	■		■	■
Group dynamics	■	■	■	■	■	■	■	■	■	■	■	■	■	■	■	■
Interpersonal skills	■	■	■	■	■	■	■	■	■	■	■	■	■	■	■	■
Leadership	■	■	■	■	■	■	■	■	■	■	■	■	■	■	■	■
Teamwork	■	■	■	■	■	■	■	■	■	■	■	■	■	■	■	■
Team-building	■	■	■	■	■	■	■	■	■	■	■	■	■	■	■	■
Listening			■		■								■		■	■
Negotiating				■	■								■		■	■
Planning	■	■		■	■	■	■	■	■	■	■	■	■	■	■	■
Problem-solving		■	■	■									■	■	■	■
Time management	■	■		■	■		■	■	■	■	■	■	■	■	■	■

CHAPTER 6

CAR PARK OR FIELD EXERCISES

1. ACROSS THE GREAT DIVIDE

Facilitator notes

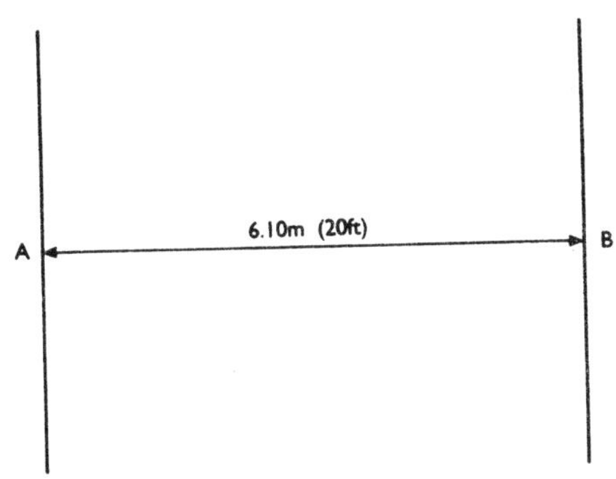

Across the Great Divide is a task in which the group has to transport a filled 25-litre (5-gall.) container from point A to point B (see above). Constraints are that the container may not touch the ground between points A and B; group members, while travelling freely between points A and B, may not touch anything except the ground whilst doing so; group members may not in any way help the task whilst they are between points A and B. An additional safety-related constraint is that neither the container nor any scaffolding poles may be thrown. The penalty for breaking any of these rules is to return the team to the start.

Numbers 4 to 8.

Time Allow 40 minutes.

Materials

To set up the task

- ☐ string/site tape
- ☐ 4 × nails or tent pegs
- ☐ 1 × surveyors' tape measure.

For group use

- ☐ 4 × 4m (12ft) alloy scaffold poles
- ☐ 4 × 2.5m (8ft) alloy scaffold poles
- ☐ 2 × 30m (100ft) 12mm polypropylene ropes
- ☐ 2 × 2m (6ft) planks
- ☐ 1 × scaffold spanner/wrench
- ☐ 1 × filled 25-litre (5-gall.) container
- ☐ climbing helmets and site gloves for all
- ☐ 16 × fixed 90° scaffold couplers
- ☐ 16 × flexible scaffold couplers.

Procedure Having set up the exercise, take the group to point A and brief either the group or the leader. Allow time for absorption and answer any amplifying questions, whilst deflecting any questions seeking ways to achieve the task. Once the questions have been dealt with, announce that the time has started and it's over to them. Review after the allowed time has elapsed or after the group has completed the task, whichever is the sooner.

Safety Safety guidelines for all scaffolding tasks are set out elsewhere (see page 47). Ensure that the group have copies, and have read and understood them.

GROUP NOTES

Across the great divide

Task To convey a filled 25-litre (5-gall.) container from area A to area B. Constraints are that the container may not touch the ground; whilst between A and B no one may help the task or touch anything but the ground; and no one may help from the sides outside the perimeter.

Equipment may not be wilfully defaced or damaged.

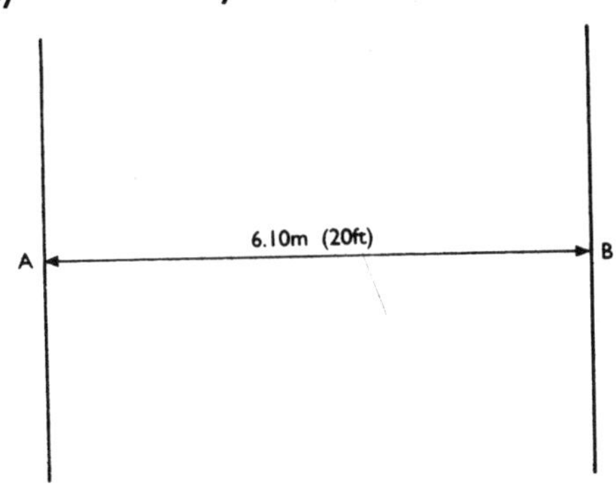

Resources

- ☐ 4 × 4m or 12ft alloy scaffold poles
- ☐ 4 × 2.5m or 8ft alloy scaffold poles
- ☐ 2 × 30m (100ft) 12mm polypropylene ropes
- ☐ 2 × 2m or 6ft planks
- ☐ 1 × scaffold spanner/wrench
- ☐ 1 × filled 25 litre (5-gall.) container
- ☐ 16 × fixed 90° scaffold couplers
- ☐ 16 × flexible scaffold couplers.
- ☐ safety helmets and site gloves for all

Time 40 minutes.

Safety The rules for safe working with scaffolding are set out on the attached sheet. Ensure that the whole group understands them before commencing the task.

2. All aloft

Facilitator notes

All Aloft is a very versatile exercise, which works well in a multi-task exercise or as a stand-alone 'grounds' event. There are elements of problem-solving and some requirement for practical skills, but it is good for teamwork and, for some reason, particularly for listening skills. Quite simply, the group have to build a structure to support themselves three feet or one metre off the ground for one minute.

Numbers 4 to 8.

Time Allow 20–30 minutes.

Materials

- ☐ 6 × 1.8m (6ft) wooden poles or beams, approx. 100mm (4in) thick
- ☐ assorted lengths of rope, at least 6, up to 1.7m long

and/or

- ☐ 3 × 1.8m (6ft) scaffold poles
- ☐ 3 × 1.2m (4ft) scaffold poles
- ☐ assorted scaffold joints
- ☐ scaffold spanner
- ☐ safety helmets and gloves for each group member.

Set-up Lay out the equipment on reasonably level ground.

Procedure Having laid out the task, take the group to the start point and brief either the group or the leader. Allow time for absorption and answer any amplifying questions whilst deflecting any questions seeking ways to achieve the task. Once the questions have been dealt with, announce that the time has started and it's over to them. Review after the allowed time has elapsed or after the group has completed the task, whichever is the sooner.

Prior training Short lessons in knot tying, lashing and use of scaffold joints may be appropriate.

Variations

- Two or more teams, side by side in competition.
- Issue no scaffolding.
- Offer extra equipment.
- Allocate a budget, a price for completion and for each item of equipment used.

Safety

- Do not allow attempts on obviously insecure structures.
- Safety guidelines for all scaffolding tasks are set out in the relevant section (see p. 47).
- Ensure that both yourself and the group have copies of the guidelines, and have read and understood them.

GROUP NOTES

All aloft

Task Your task is to build a structure that will support your entire team 1m (3ft) off the ground for one minute. The structure must be free standing. It may not be leaned against anything or be held together by team members.

Resources

- ☐ 6 × 1.8m (6ft) wooden poles or beams, approx. 100mm (4in) thick
- ☐ assorted lengths of rope, at least 6, up to 1.7m long
- ☐ 3 × 1.8m scaffold poles
- ☐ 3 × 1.2m scaffold poles
- ☐ assorted scaffold joints
- ☐ scaffold spanner
- ☐ safety helmets and gloves for each group member.

Time 30 minutes.

You may only use the equipment provided.

The minute will be timed by your facilitator. You must tell him/her when you are ready.

Safety

- The rules for safe working with scaffolding are set out on the attached sheet. Ensure that the whole group understands them before commencing the task.
- Tutors' rulings on matters of safety are final and binding.
- No one may jump from any structure you build.
- Safety helmets and gloves will be worn.
- Be aware of the need for safe working practices at all times.

3. Ankles away

Facilitator notes

Ankles Away is a quick and simple exercise which is a very good ice-breaker, requiring total co-operation and a lot of mutual support. It involves the group moving along a predetermined route, with their ankles tied together. It should be briefed *verbally*.

Numbers 4 to 8.

Time Allow 10–20 minutes.

Materials

- ☐ Enough 'ties' for each group member.

Procedure

1. Decide on and check the route.
2. Issue the ties and have each team member tie their left leg to another's right leg.
3. The circle may be complete or with two 'free legs'. (Tutor decides or allows interpretation by group, dependent on objectives.)
4. Brief the group on the route and explain that they may not remove the ties until they have finished.

Variation Two teams, with a route requiring them to pass each other in a confined space, such as a hotel corridor.

Safety Cover the group when negotiating any obstacles, such as steps.

4. Bipod bipeds

Facilitator notes

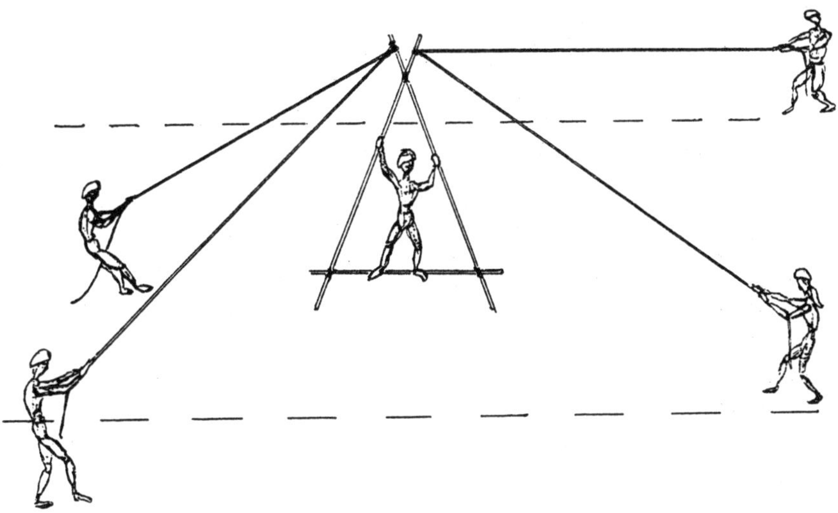

Bipod Bipeds is a multi-group task, the purpose of which is to 'walk' triangular scaffolding structures across a 6.10m (20ft) gap. In effect the exercise is a race, either between groups or against time. Four team members (who may not touch the structure) hold ropes which are attached to it, whilst a fifth stands upon it and acts as the 'driver'. A sixth group member can act as coordinator. This is illustrated above.

Numbers 5 or 6 per group.

Time Allow 30 minutes for building and practising, with a further 15–20 minutes for the race phase. As a great deal of space is taken up by the bipeds and their crews, it may be necessary to organize heats or, in circumstances of limited space, run it as a 'time trial' event.

Materials

To set up the task

- ☐ string/site tape
- ☐ 4 × nails or tent pegs
- ☐ 1 × surveyors' tape measure.

For group use (per group)

- ☐ 2 × 4m (12ft) alloy scaffold poles
- ☐ 1 × 2.5m (8ft) alloy scaffold pole
- ☐ 2 × 30m (100ft) 12mm polypropylene ropes
- ☐ 1 × scaffold spanner/wrench
- ☐ 3 × flexible scaffold couplers
- ☐ safety helmets and site gloves for all.

Procedure Having set up the exercise, take the group to the start point and give either the group or the leader the brief. Allow time for absorption and answer any amplifying questions whilst deflecting any questions seeking tips on achieving the task. Once the questions have been dealt with, announce that the planning/building time has started and it's over to them. Ensure their tripods conform with the specification in their brief. Review after the races are finished and winners declared.

Prior training Although none is strictly necessary, the exercise works best if delegates have completed another scaffolding exercise beforehand, and become accustomed to the materials.

Safety Although the task seems to pose some risks, it is surprisingly free from danger, provided proper precautions are observed. Ensure that:

- team members holding ropes always stand at a greater distance than the length of the longest scaffold pole;
- all wear helmets and gloves;
- the 'passenger' calls the shots, and is comfortably able to step on and off the cross piece, which should be no further than 30cm (1ft) from the ground;
- all scaffold couplers are well secured;
- arrange for staff to be available and monitoring on a ratio of one per team.

GROUP NOTES

Bipod bipeds

Task To build and race scaffolding bipods with the objective of winning a race/time trial. Four group members may hold ropes, a fifth should act as 'passenger' (see diagram). Further group members are limited to an 'advice and encouragement' role. When racing, the bipod must be 'mounted' at all times. If the rider steps down or falls off, the bipod must return to the start. Bipods must conform to the diagram.

Resources

- ☐ 2 × 4m (12ft) alloy scaffold poles
- ☐ 1 × 2.5m (8ft) alloy scaffold pole
- ☐ 2 × 30m (100ft) 12mm polypropylene ropes
- ☐ 1 × scaffold spanner/wrench
- ☐ 3 × flexible scaffold couplers
- ☐ safety helmets and site gloves for all.

Time 30 minutes to build the bipods and practice racing them before the inter-group scaffold-driving competition.

Building scaffolding bipods

Step 1 Build these using 3 flexible scaffolding couplers, 2 × 4m (12ft) scaffolding poles and 1 × 2.5m (8ft) scaffolding pole.

Step 2 Affix the *centre* of a 30m (100ft) rope to each 'horn' of the bipod, with a team member holding each of the four ropes thus formed. Place a fifth team member on the bipod (see diagram).

Step 3 By pulling and slackening the ropes, 'walk' the bipod across the race route.

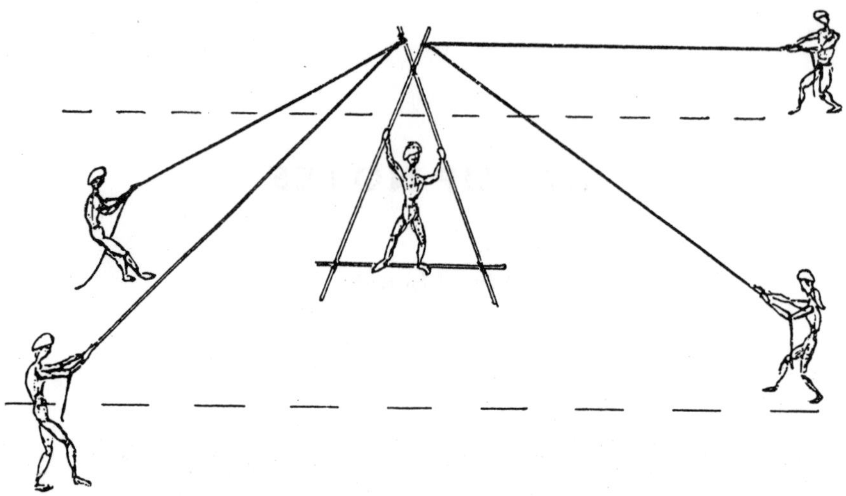

Safety Ensure that:

- team members holding ropes always stand at a greater distance than the length of the longest scaffold pole;
- all wear helmets and gloves;
- the 'passenger' calls the shots, and is comfortably able to step on and off the cross piece, which should be no further than 30cm (1ft) from the ground;
- all scaffold couplers are well secured.

Staff rulings on all safety matters are final and binding.

5. Blind intent

Facilitator notes

Blind Intent is an exercise in which the group has to erect a small tent, with all but one of their number blindfolded.

Numbers The minimum number is about 4. The maximum depends on the size of the tent. The exercise has been run with 12 participants, erecting a large 6-person ridge tent. Family camping tents are not appropriate for this exercise as even without blindfolds they are extremely difficult to erect.

Time 45 minutes.

Materials

- ☐ blindfolds for group
- ☐ tent including poles and guy ropes
- ☐ tent pegs/meat skewers
- ☐ 2 mallets (preferably rubber).

Procedure Lay out the equipment on the piece of ground to be used, conduct the group to the site and hand out the brief. Do not allow people to touch the tent or hardware until the group has requested for all but one to be blindfolded and this has been done to your satisfaction.

Whilst tent pitching is taking place, watch out for the safety points listed below. The exercise is complete either at the closedown time or when the group have completed the job, whichever is the sooner.

Safety Most people are very cautious when they are blindfolded. Nevertheless, observe for:

- people in danger of walking into each other;
- irresponsible use of tent poles;
- irresponsible use of mallets.

In all cases intervene quietly on a one-to-one basis with the people concerned.

GROUP NOTES

Blind intent

Task To erect the tent which we have provided. There is a complication: only people who are effectively blindfolded may touch the tent or its components. Once one person dons a blindfold, all but one of the group must do likewise. The person who is not blindfolded *may not* touch the tent. Once donned, blindfolds must be worn by the tent-touchers for the whole time, or whatever shorter time it takes to erect the tent.

Resources Only the materials provided.

Time 45 minutes.

Safety Staff in attendance have final authority in safety-related matters.

6. Blue peter

Facilitator notes

Blue Peter is a problem-solving exercise requiring some creativity and practicality, but no physical prowess; it also requires some coordination of effort as the task is effectively two connected ones. The task is simply to design, build and erect a flagpole to fly the group's own flag.

Numbers 4 to 8.

Time Allow 20–30 minutes.

Materials

- ☐ 20 garden canes, ranging from 4 to 8ft long
- ☐ Sellotape
- ☐ string
- ☐ scissors
- ☐ 6 × tent pegs
- ☐ flag-making materials, such as:
  - cloth
  - paint or pens
  - needle and strong thread.

Set-up Lay out the equipment in an area large enough to manoeuvre long and tall structures. Remember height clearance as well as width!

Procedure Having laid out the task, take the group to the start point and brief either the group or the leader. Allow time for absorption and answer any amplifying questions whilst deflecting any questions seeking ways to achieve the task. Once the questions have been dealt with, announce that the time has started and it's over to them. Review after the allowed time has elapsed or after the group has completed the task, whichever is the sooner.

Variation Two or more teams, side by side in competition, with points for flag design and flagstaff height.

Safety Watch for canes being waved carelessly about. Ensure care when erecting.

GROUP NOTES

Blue Peter

Task To design and make a team flag, and to erect a flagstaff from which to fly it. The flag should show your team name and logo, which should reflect the team's identity and values. The flagstaff must be freestanding and at least 20 feet or 6m high.

Resources

- ☐ assorted garden canes (not be broken or stuck in the ground)
- ☐ Sellotape
- ☐ string
- ☐ scissors
- ☐ 6 × tent pegs
- ☐ cloth
- ☐ paint or pens
- ☐ needle and strong thread.

Time 30 minutes.

Safety Be aware of the need for safe working practices at all times.

7. Container ferry

Facilitator notes

Container Ferry is a task in which the group change the balance of water containers attached to each other by a rope which passes via pulley wheels through a 'T' shaped scaffolding structure so that water container 'A', which is initially up in the air, touches the ground, whilst container 'B' moves up into the air. Constraints are that only the equipment provided may be used, nothing except masking tape may be deliberately broken, and nothing and no one may touch anything (other than the air) in a zone around the structure. This is illustrated below (diagram not to scale):

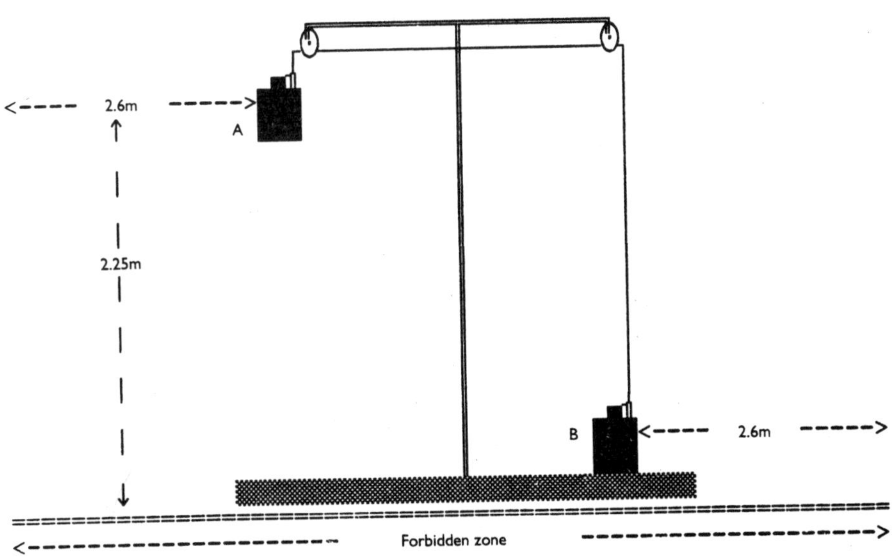

Numbers 4 to 6.

Time Allow 20 minutes.

Materials

To set up the task

- ☐ 1 × 2.40m (8ft) alloy scaffold pole
- ☐ 1 × 1.20m (4ft) alloy scaffold pole
- ☐ 1 × fixed 90° scaffold clip
- ☐ 1 × scaffold spanner
- ☐ 4.20m (14ft) 5mm polypropylene rope
- ☐ 2 × pulley wheels, capable of being attached to the scaffolding by string
- ☐ string for the above
- ☐ 2 × 25-litre (5-gall.) water containers
- ☐ 1 × base for the scaffolding structure
- ☐ string/site tape
- ☐ 4 × tent pegs/nails.

For group use

- ☐ sundry pipes making a total length of 2.6m
- ☐ 1 × 1.20m (4ft) plastic drainpipe
- ☐ 1 × 0.85m (3ft) plastic drainpipe
- ☐ 3 × plastic mugs
- ☐ 1 × full reel masking tape
- ☐ 4.20m (14ft) 5mm polypropylene rope
- ☐ 1 large bucket of water.

Procedure Having set up the exercise, take the group to a point close to it and give either the group or the leader the brief. Allow a few minutes for the group to digest it, answering amplifying questions but pushing back to the groups any questions seeking clues as to how to do the task. After questions, announce the time has started, and it's over to them.

Safety Ensure that anyone volunteering to lift people does not suffer from back-related problems, and that they lift correctly, keeping the back straight and bending the legs. Depute other group members to assist in the lifting and lowering process.

Stand in front of any multi-person structure, and depute a group member to stand behind. Both of you should be ready to assist should the human structure show signs of collapsing.

Set-up

1. Connect the scaffold poles so that the 1.20m (4ft) pole forms the cross of a 'T' with the 2.40m (8ft) pole forming the tail. Ensure the scaffold clip is secured as tightly as possible, using the spanner to tighten it.
2. Tie a pulley wheel tightly to each end of the 1.20m (4ft) pole.
3. Thread the 5mm polypropylene rope through the pulleys, ensuring that it runs smoothly.
4. Remove the cap from both 25-litre (5-gallon) containers.
5. Move the assembly into the vertical position and secure firmly. We usually use a wooden base made from 25cm × 5cm (9in. × 2in.) wood, securely screwed together with a wooden upright 50cm (1ft 7in.) piece of wood which fits securely inside the scaffold pole (to achieve this see diagram below). On occasions we have merely 'guyed' the structure securely upright. A plan of the base, well within the abilities of any D.I.Y. enthusiast or carpenter, is set out below.
6. Tie the 25-litre containers to each end of the rope and haul into position as in the diagram below. 'Lose' any spare rope inside a container.
7. Lay out and secure the string/site tape so that the boundary thus formed is at least 2.60m (7ft 6in.) from the higher 25-litre container.
8. Ensure that the group's equipment is to hand and the bucket is filled.

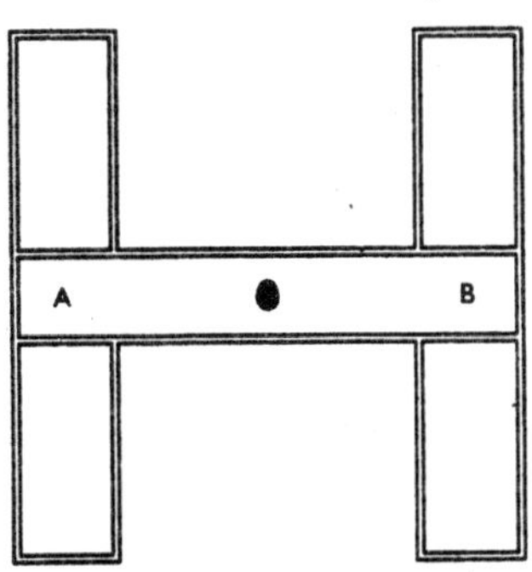

Wooden base: from above

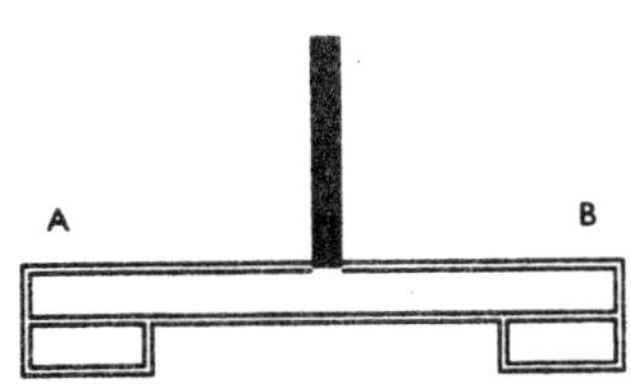

Wooden base: side view

All planks 25cm × 5cm (9in. × 2in.) and 1.15m (4ft) long, secured by 5 screws at point A and point B.

GROUP NOTES

Container ferry

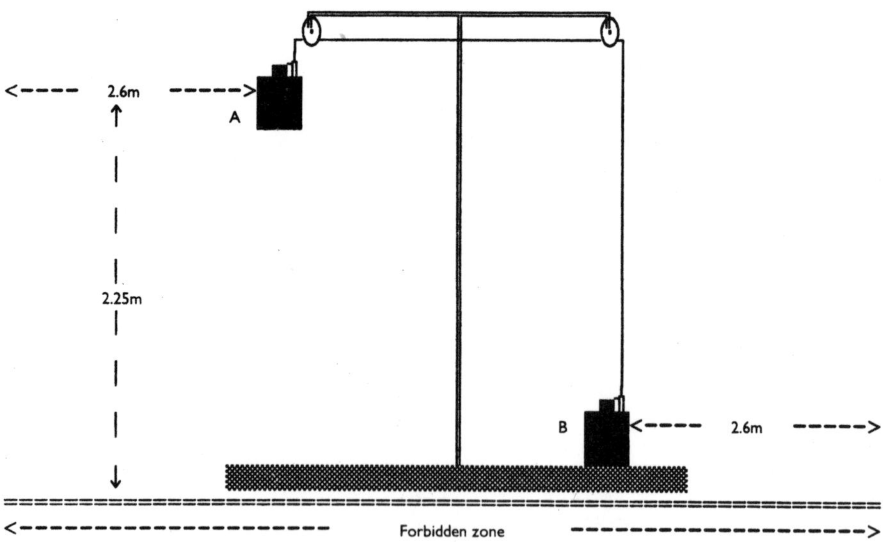

Task To change the balance of the water containers so that container A touches the ground and container B is up in the air. Constraints are that only the equipment provided may be used, and no one and nothing except water may touch anything except the air inside the forbidden zone.

Equipment may not be wilfully defaced or damaged.

Resources

- ☐ 1 × 1.20m (4ft) plastic drainpipe
- ☐ 1 × 0.85m (3ft) plastic drainpipe
- ☐ 3 × plastic mugs
- ☐ 1 × full reel masking tape
- ☐ 1 × 4.20m (14ft) 5mm polypropylene rope
- ☐ 1 large bucket of water.

Time 20 minutes.

Safety If any lifting of heavy weights is required, consult with your trainer for correct methods before proceeding. Be aware of the need for safe working practices at all times.

8. Credibility gap

Facilitator notes

Credibility Gap is a task in which the group travels from area A to area B (see below) taking with it a filled 25-litre (5-gall.) water container. To make the task achievable, and to build in an added complication to communication, one member may be placed at area B after the initial planning stage but before the action phase. Other constraints are that no one may go around the obstacle, nothing and nobody may touch the ground between A and B, and the container and poles may not be thrown across the gap between A and B. The penalty for breaking any of these rules is for the team to return to the start.

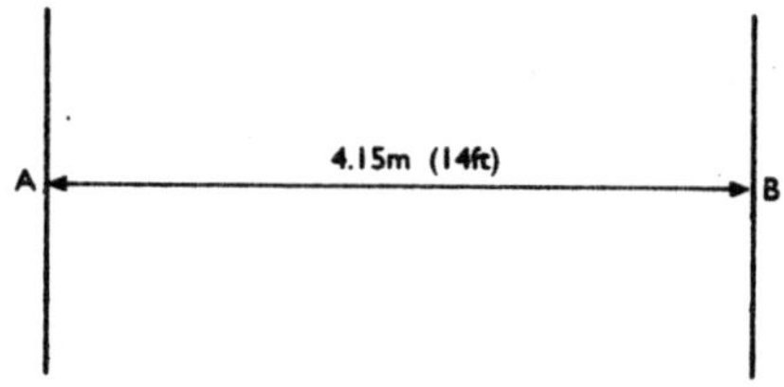

Numbers 4 to 8.

Time Allow 40 minutes.

Materials

To set up the task

- ☐ string/site tape
- ☐ 4 × nails or tent pegs
- ☐ 1 × surveyors' tape measure.

For group use

At point A:

- ☐ 3 × 4m (12ft) alloy scaffold poles
- ☐ 30m (100ft) 12mm polypropylene rope
- ☐ 1 × scaffold spanner/wrench
- ☐ 1 × filled 25-litre (5-gall.) container
- ☐ safety helmets and site gloves for all.

At point B:

- ☐ 2 × 4m (12ft) alloy scaffold poles
- ☐ 16 × fixed 90° scaffold couplers
- ☐ 16 × flexible scaffold couplers
- ☐ 30m (100ft) 12mm polypropylene rope.

Procedure Having set up the exercise, take the group to point A and brief either the group or the leader. Allow time for absorption and answer any amplifying questions whilst deflecting any questions seeking ways to achieve the task. Ensure they understand that they may place a person at point B but that, once placed, they must remain on that side of the boundary string/site tape. After all this is understood, announce that the time has started and it's over to them.

Safety Safety guidelines for all scaffolding tasks are set out in the relevant chapter (see page 47). Ensure that both yourself and the group have copies, and have read and understood them.

GROUP NOTES

Credibility gap

Task For the whole group and a filled 25-litre (5-gall.) container to travel from area A to area B. The main constraint is that nothing and no one may touch the ground in the taped-off area between A and B. In addition, no one may walk around the area.

One person may be placed in area B before the 'hands-on' phase of the task commences, but once placed there, may not return to area A. The rule about not touching the ground between A and B also applies to this group member.

Equipment may not be wilfully defaced or damaged.

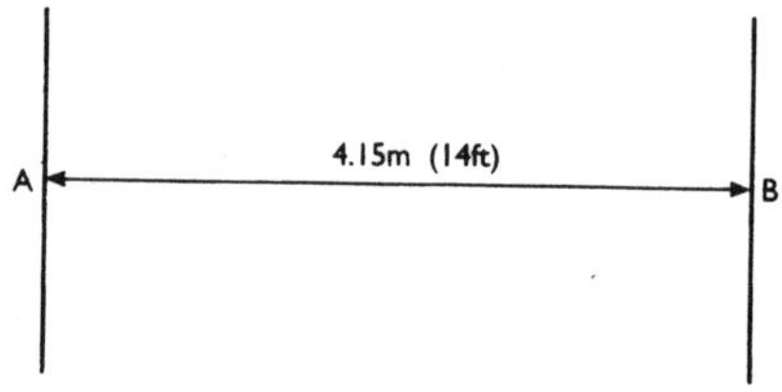

Resources

At point A

- ☐ 3 × 4m (12ft) alloy scaffold poles
- ☐ 1 × 30m (100ft) 12mm polypropylene rope
- ☐ 1 × scaffold spanner/wrench
- ☐ 1 × filled 25-litre (5-gall.) container
- ☐ safety helmets and site gloves for all.

At point B

- ☐ 2 × 4m (12ft) alloy scaffold poles
- ☐ 16 × fixed 90° scaffold couplers
- ☐ 16 × flexible scaffold couplers
- ☐ 1 × 30m (100ft) 12mm polypropylene rope.

Time 40 minutes.

Safety The rules for safe working with scaffolding are set out on the attached sheet. Ensure that the whole group understands them before commencing the task.

9. Design of the Times

Facilitator notes

Design of the Times is an excellent exercise for helping groups to focus on process needs, whilst at the same time helping them to exercise creativity.

The task requires two groups who have either been working together on a course for a number of days or who interact in the working environment. The exercise is in four phases:

Phase 1 Through discussion, to arrive at a consensus as to the area that requires greatest improvement for them as a team and share this information with another group who, in their turn, do the same.

Phase 2 To design and set up a lightweight outdoor exercise to help the other group address their area of need.

Phase 3 To observe the other group doing that exercise, and run a review with them.

Phase 4 To undertake a lightweight outdoor exercise which the other group has designed and set up for them, and jointly review it together afterwards.

Phases 3 and 4 are, of course, interchangeable, and usually decided by the toss of a coin.

Numbers 4 to 8 per group.

Time 190 minutes, broken up as follows:

Phase 1 45 minutes

Phase 2 60 minutes

Phases 3 and 4 85 minutes (40 minutes per exercise/review plus 5 minutes' changeover time)

Equipment Allow groups to take as required from available stocks of scaffolding rope, planks, etc.

Procedure Issue briefs to groups in separate rooms. Act as go-between at the closing stages of phase 1, then allow the exercise to continue through phases 2–4, ensuring you are present at reviews, keeping them objective and process-focused, but intervening as little as possible.

Prior Training The exercise works best after groups have completed a number of lightweight outdoor exercises and have some understanding of the learning potential and equipment available.

Variations The exercise can be used in courses with any multiple of two groups.

Safety Physical safety depends on what the groups design. In all cases offer the services of a safety tutor to each group to comment on safety matters, with authority to overrule.

GROUP NOTES

Design of the times

Task A four-phase exercise in which you are required to exercise analytical and creative skills.

Phase 1 In this phase you should discuss and come to a consensus on what you believe to be your group's area requiring greatest improvement when working as a team. When you have agreed this, you should write it down and pass it to a member of staff who will take it on to the other group. You will receive a note from them setting down what they believe to be their area requiring greatest improvement.

You have 45 minutes for this phase.

Phase 2 You design an exercise of a maximum 20 minutes' duration, aimed at helping the other group to address the training need which they have expressed in their note. This exercise should be difficult but achievable in the time allowed.

You have 60 minutes to do this.

Phase 3 On the toss of a coin, one group performs the exercise designed by the other group, whilst they observe. Observing groups should concentrate on watching for:

- behaviour which helps the group doing the exercise to overcome the problem it has identified;
- behaviour which may cause or magnify problems in the identified area.

After the task has been completed or the allowed time has elapsed, the observing group should conduct a review (maximum 20 minutes) with the task group. They should conduct this review as far as possible by:

- asking open questions (e.g. 'How did it go?' or 'In what ways did it go better/worse than you expected?');
- probing the responses (e.g. 'Why do you think this was?');
- seeking *for the task group* to articulate its conclusions (e.g. 'So what can be learned from the way the task was performed?').

Do not tell people what they learned or speculate why they acted in a particular way. Ask them!

Phase 4 As Phase 3, with groups exchanging roles.

Resources You may use any equipment available from stock for this exercise, but tell course staff what you require.

Safety A member of safety staff is available to your group. You may consult her/him on all safety related matters and s/he will anyway volunteer advice in this area. As in all exercises, staff have the authority to veto anything on grounds of safety. Safety staff will also monitor safe performance of tasks.

10. First service

Facilitator notes

First Service is a problem-solving exercise requiring some creativity and practicality, but no physical prowess. The task is simply to design and build a launching device for a tennis ball. (The most common and most successful is some form of catapult.)

Numbers 4 to 8.

Time Allow 20–30 minutes.

Materials

- ☐ 10 garden canes, ranging from 4 to 8ft long
- ☐ Sellotape
- ☐ string
- ☐ plastic cup
- ☐ assorted elastic bands
- ☐ scissors
- ☐ plastic funnel
- ☐ 2 × tent pegs
- ☐ tennis ball.

Set-up Lay out the equipment, ensuring sufficient target area.

Procedure Having laid out the task, take the group to the start point and brief either the group or the leader. Avoid answering unnecessary questions or giving overhelpful or limiting clarification. (Typical are comments like 'So we have to build a . . .') Ensure that the constraints are adhered to. The reference in the group notes to 'human contact' is intended to encourage the design, preparation and use of a trigger device, such as string being cut.

Variations Two or more teams, side by side in competition. The furthest throw wins. Target area to land the ball in.

Safety

- Watch for canes being waved carelessly about.
- Ensure care when launching, taking particular note of pieces other than the tennis ball flying, e.g. the tent peg!
- Ensure that people do not stand in front of any loaded launching device.

GROUP NOTES

First service

Task Your task is to build a structure or machine to propel a tennis ball over a horizontal distance of 50 feet. There is to be no direct human contact with the machine during launching.

Resources

- ☐ assorted garden canes (These must not be broken or stuck in the ground.)
- ☐ Sellotape
- ☐ string
- ☐ plastic cup
- ☐ assorted elastic bands
- ☐ scissors
- ☐ plastic funnel
- ☐ 2 × tent pegs
- ☐ tennis ball

Time 30 minutes.

11. Going the Distance

Facilitator notes

Going the Distance is a physically lightweight task in which the group is given a brief and a selection of materials, and has to devise and demonstrate a way of transporting a table-tennis ball the maximum distance possible. Constraints are that they must build a mechanical or aeronautical device, not merely throw it. They may make as many attempts as they wish within the rules and the time constraints.

Numbers 4 to 7 per group, with preferably more than one group doing the task at once.

Time Allow 45 or 50 minutes.

Materials

To set up the task

- ☐ string/site tape (to define the start-point)
- ☐ 4 × nails/tent pegs
- ☐ surveyors' tape measure (for measuring attempts).

For group use (per group)

- ☐ 1 × table tennis ball
- ☐ 5 × small plastic bags
- ☐ 1 × reel of sticky tape
- ☐ 20 × sheets of tissue paper (A2 or A3 size)
- ☐ 1 × ball of li[illegible]eight string
- ☐ 3 × bootlaces

- ☐ 1 × metal coat hanger
- ☐ 1 × piece of Blu Tack
- ☐ 1 × camping gas or meths cooker, with dry matches and fuel
- ☐ 10 × 45cm (1ft 6in.) plant sticks
- ☐ 1 × jamjar of wallpaper glue (pre-mixed)
- ☐ 5 × waste sacks
- ☐ about 100 × elastic bands
- ☐ 12 × sheets A4 copying paper
- ☐ 1 × 2m (6ft) length of plastic piping.

Procedure Set up the line for the start-point in a large area (soccer field or large lawn), take the groups to the start-point and brief either the leaders or the groups. Allow time for any amplifying questions whilst deflecting anything already covered in the brief or seeking a solution to the problem. After questions, announce that the time has started, and it's over to them.

Safety There are no major safety issues in this task, but ensure that people are aware of how to use meths cookers (sometimes these are available cheaply as picnic stoves from traditional ironmongers, sometimes expensively as Trangias from outdoor suppliers). An old blanket at hand is a good idea should the cooker be over-fuelled. Always keep meths stored away from the flame, and do not allow people to attempt to refuel a lighted cooker. Primus-type stoves should be avoided as they are complicated and produce a very hot, fierce flame.

GROUP NOTES

Going the distance

Task To devise and demonstrate a way of transporting a table-tennis ball the maximum distance possible. You must build a mechanical or aeronautical device, not merely throw it. You may make as many attempts as you wish within the rules and the time constraints.

Resources

- ☐ 1 × table tennis ball
- ☐ 5 × small plastic bags
- ☐ 1 × reel of sticky tape
- ☐ 20 × sheets of tissue paper (A2 or A3 size)
- ☐ 1 × ball of lightweight string
- ☐ 3 × bootlaces
- ☐ 1 × metal coat hanger
- ☐ 1 × piece of Blu Tack
- ☐ 1 × camping gas or meths cooker, with dry matches and fuel
- ☐ 10 × 45cm (1ft 6in.) plant sticks
- ☐ 1 × jamjar of wallpaper glue (pre-mixed)
- ☐ 5 × waste sacks
- ☐ about 100 × elastic bands
- ☐ 12 × sheets A4 copying paper
- ☐ 1 × 2m (6ft) length of plastic piping.

Time 50 minutes.

Safety Seek staff advice before lighting the cooker. Be aware of the need for safe working practices at all times.

12. JAM TOMORROW

Facilitator notes

Jam Tomorrow is a task in which the group retrieve a jamjar from a 'forbidden zone' without either themselves or their equipment touching the ground within that zone.

Numbers 3 to 6.

Time Allow 15 minutes.

Materials

To set up the task

- ☐ string/site tape to define the zone
- ☐ tent pegs/nails to secure the string/tape
- ☐ a 454g (1lb) jar of jam.

For group use

- ☐ 3 × 10m (33ft) 5–7mm polypropylene ropes
- ☐ a large box of elastic bands (various sizes and widths)
- ☐ a reel of adhesive tape
- ☐ 4 tent pegs.

Set-up Lay out and secure the string/site tape as shown in the diagram (not to scale). The jamjar (marked ★) should be laid in the centre of the large square.

Procedure Having set up the exercise, take the group to a point close

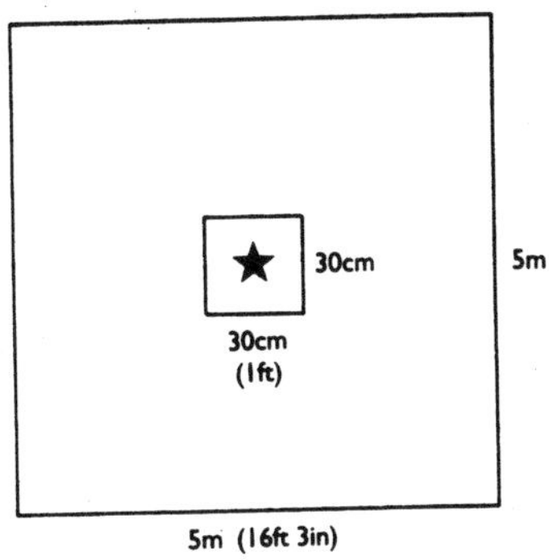

to the layout and brief either the group or the leader, answering any amplifying questions but pushing back to the group any questions seeking clues as to how to do the task. After questions, announce the time has started, and it's over to them.

Prior training None required.

Safety There are no major safety matters to take into account with this exercise.

GROUP NOTES

Jam tomorrow

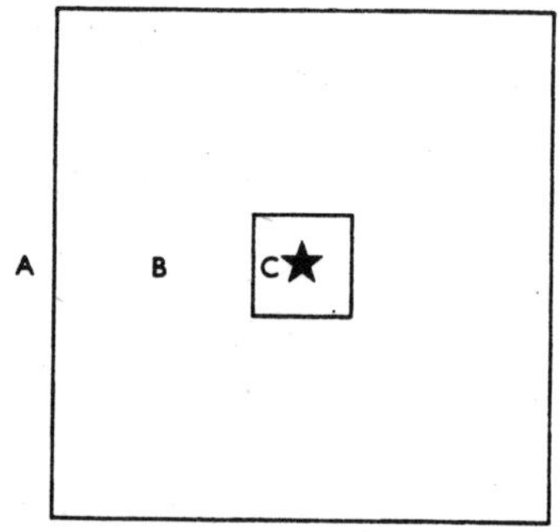

Task to retrieve the jamjar (marked ★ on the diagram) from area C, and bring it back to area A. Nothing and no one may touch the ground in area B.

Resources

- ☐ 3 × 10m (33ft) 5–7mm polypropylene ropes
- ☐ a large box of elastic bands (various sizes and widths)
- ☐ a reel of adhesive tape
- ☐ 4 × tent-pegs

You may not supplement this equipment.

Time 15 minutes.

Safety You must comply with any safety inputs from your trainer, and remain conscious of the need for safe working at all times.

13. PLAYING A BLINDER

Facilitator notes

Playing a Blinder is a variation on *Jam Tomorrow,* with the added variation that all but one of the team is blindfolded. This makes it a considerably more difficult task.

Numbers 3 to 6.

Time Allow 30 minutes.

Materials

To set up the task

- ☐ string/site tape to define the zone
- ☐ tent pegs/nails to secure the string/tape
- ☐ 1 × 454g (1lb) jar of jam
- ☐ blindfolds for all but one of the group.

For group use

- ☐ 3 × 10m (33ft) 5–7mm polypropylene ropes
- ☐ a large box of elastic bands (various sizes and widths)
- ☐ a reel of adhesive tape
- ☐ 4 × tent pegs.

Set-up As for *Jam Tomorrow.*

Procedure Having set up the exercise and cleared the ground of any moveable hazards, take the group to a point close to the layout and announce that in this task all but one are to be blindfolded.

Allow the group to agree who is to remain sighted, and, once they have done so, blindfold the rest and brief the sighted one. Allow that person a few minutes to digest the brief. Answer any amplifying questions, pushing back any seeking clues as to how to do the task. After questions, announce the time has started, and it's over to them.

Do not allow blindfolds to be removed (except for health and safety reasons) until either the time runs out or the task is completed, whichever is the sooner. At that point, retire to review.

Safety Although there are no particular safety matters to take into account, any task in which people are blindfolded can lead to them walking into any obstacles, including each other. Maintain alertness and quietly intervene before people move into danger.

GROUP NOTES

Playing a blinder

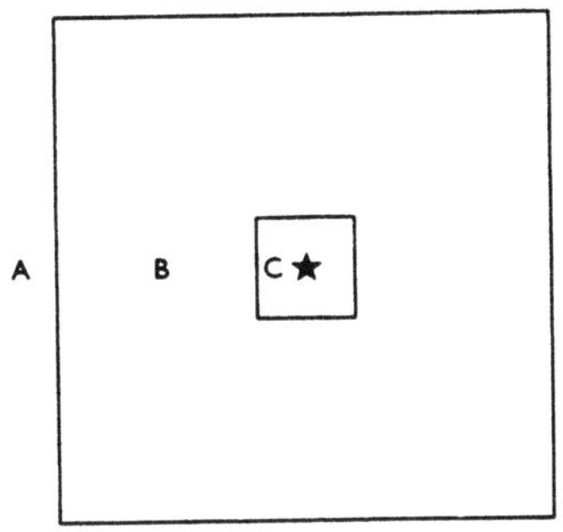

Task To retrieve the jamjar (marked ★ on the diagram) from area C, and bring it back to area A. Nothing and no one may touch the ground in area B. All the team except one member must remain blindfolded for the duration of the task. The person who is not blindfolded may not touch any equipment.

Resources

- ☐ 3 × 10m (33ft) 5–7mm polypropylene ropes
- ☐ a large box of elastic bands (various sizes and widths)
- ☐ a reel of adhesive tape
- ☐ 4 × tent pegs.

You may not supplement this equipment.

Time 30 minutes.

Safety Be aware of the need to ensure that wherever blindfolded people walk, they avoid human and inanimate obstacles. In addition, you must comply with any safety inputs from your trainer, and remain conscious of the need for safe working at all times.

14. Poacher's Escape

Facilitator notes

Poacher's Escape is a task with a purpose which is more complex than at first seems: for the whole group and a bucket of water to travel from area A to area D without either themselves, their bucket, or their equipment touching the ground between A and B or between C and D, and *without anything touching the trestle fence*. Group members, the equipment, and the bucket may touch the ground between B and C.

Numbers 4 to 6.

Time Allow 40 minutes.

Materials

To set up the task

- ☐ 2 × adjustable steel decorator's trestles
- ☐ polythene sheeting to cover the trestles
- ☐ string or site-tape to designate boundaries
- ☐ tent pegs/nails and a mallet to secure strings/tape

For group use

- ☐ bucket of water
- ☐ 1 × 1.70m (6ft) plank with a 12mm (½in.) hole drilled near one end
- ☐ 2 × 30m (100ft) lengths of 10mm (⅜in.) polypropylene rope
- ☐ 1 × 1.70m (6ft) ladder (a stepladder tied in the closed position will do)

- ☐ 2 × 25-gallon drums
- ☐ notebook and pen/pencil
- ☐ safety helmet for each group member
- ☐ gardening gloves for each group member

Set-up *Poacher's Escape* and *Passover*. Both tasks are set up in the following manner:

Erect the decorator's trestles side by side, to a height approximately between the chest and midriff, and drape with polythene, which should then be anchored to the ground.

Ensure that any pieces of the trestle which jut out and might cause injury are suitably 'masked'. We find that a tennis ball sliced and placed over them is suitable.

Lay out the site tape/string, pegged/nailed in each corner, as shown below:

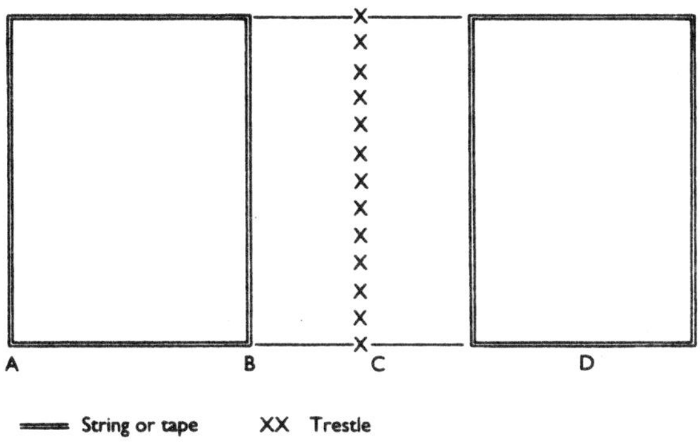

Poacher's Escape: diagram of layout

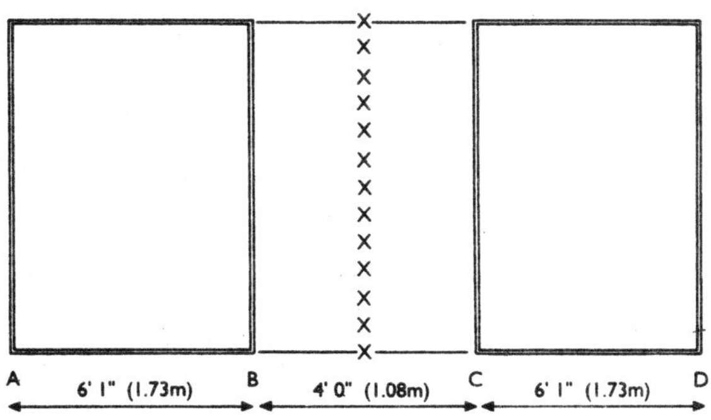

Poacher's Escape: dimensions

Procedure Having set up the exercise, take the group to a position around point A, where their equipment should be awaiting them, and brief either the group or the leader. Answer any amplifying questions but push back to the group any questions seeking clues as to how to do the task. After five minutes, announce the time has started, and it's over to them. Review after the given time or when the group has completed the task, whichever is the sooner.

Safety

- Ensure that group members wear safety helmets and gardening gloves. The former are important when planks are being lifted at head height, the latter to protect from splinters.
- Discourage solutions which require people to jump from a height greater than one metre. Even a small jump can lead to fractured limbs or twisted joints.
- Take care when delegates are crossing the fence, and ensure that a safety tutor is close enough to catch anyone falling.

GROUP NOTES

Poacher's escape

Task The whole group and a bucket of water must travel from area A to area D without the group, the bucket or the equipment touching the ground between A and B or C and D, and without either yourselves, the bucket, or your equipment touching the fence. You and your equipment *may* touch the ground between B and C. The penalty for breaking the rules is for the whole team, the bucket, and the equipment to return to the start.

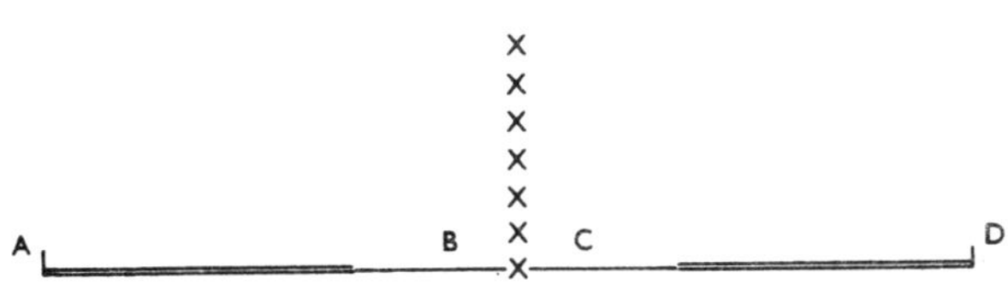

Poacher's Escape: cross section of layout.

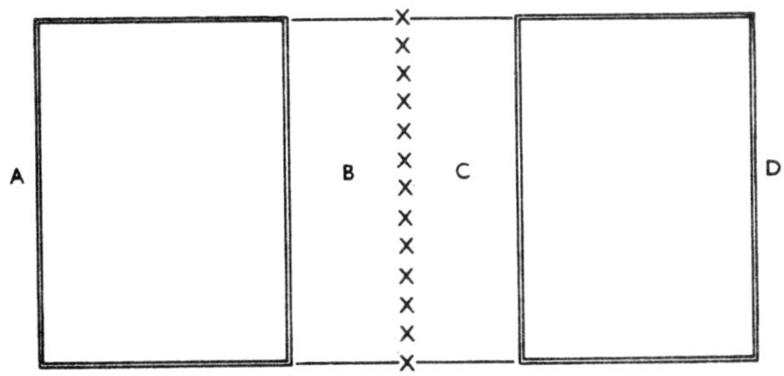

Poacher's Escape: ground-plan of set-up.

Resources

- ☐ bucket of water
- ☐ 1 × 1.70m (6ft) plank with a 12mm (½in.) hole drilled near one end
- ☐ 2 × 30m (100ft) 10mm (⅜in.) polypropylene ropes
- ☐ 1 × 1.70m (6ft) ladder
- ☐ 2 × 125-litre (25-gall.) drums
- ☐ notebook and pen/pencil
- ☐ safety helmet for each group member
- ☐ gardening gloves for each group member

Time 40 minutes.

Safety

- Tutors' rulings on safety matters are final and binding.
- No one may jump from a height greater than one metre.
- Helmets and gloves must be worn.

15. Passover

Facilitator notes

Passover is a two-group variation of *Poacher's Escape*, particularly useful when inter-group co-operation is being sought, or when numbers greater than six are involved. One group has a brief to move from A to D, whilst the other travels from D to A. Equipment is divided between the groups (see separate briefs). Rules for each group are as for *Poacher's Escape*. Note that the group briefs are silent on the matter of co-operation, which thus becomes an issue for the groups to deal with.

Numbers 4 to 6 per group, preferably in equal numbers.

Time Allow 40 minutes.

Materials

To set up the task
As for *Poacher's Escape*.

For group 1 (near point A)

- ☐ 1 × 1.70m (6ft) plank
- ☐ 1 × 125-litre (25-gall.) container
- ☐ 1 × 30m (100ft) rope
- ☐ 1 × bucket of water
- ☐ notebook and pen/pencil
- ☐ safety helmet for each group member
- ☐ gardening gloves for each member.

For group 2 (near point D)

- ☐ 1 × 1.70m (6ft) plank
- ☐ 1 × 125-litre (25-gall.) container
- ☐ 1 × 1.70m (6ft) ladder
- ☐ 1 × 30m (100ft) rope
- ☐ 1 × bucket of water
- ☐ notebook and pen/pencil
- ☐ safety helmet for each group member
- ☐ gardening gloves for each member.

Procedure Having set up the exercise, take the groups to their respective positions around points A and D, where their equipment should be awaiting them, and brief either the groups or their leaders. Allow a few minutes for the groups to digest the briefs. Answer any amplifying questions but push back to the group any questions seeking clues as to how to do the task or regarding their relationship with the other group. After five minutes, announce the time has started, and it's over to them. Review after the given time or when the groups have completed the task, whichever is the sooner.

Prior training No prior training is needed for this task, but an input on the necessity for safety wear and safe working is useful.

Safety As for *Poacher's Escape.*

GROUP I NOTES

Passover

Task The whole group and a bucket of water travel from area A to area D without the group, the bucket or the equipment touching the ground between A and B or C and D, and without either yourselves, the bucket, or your equipment touching the fence. You and your equipment *may* touch the ground between B and C. The penalty for breaking the rules is for the whole team, the bucket, and the equipment to return to the start.

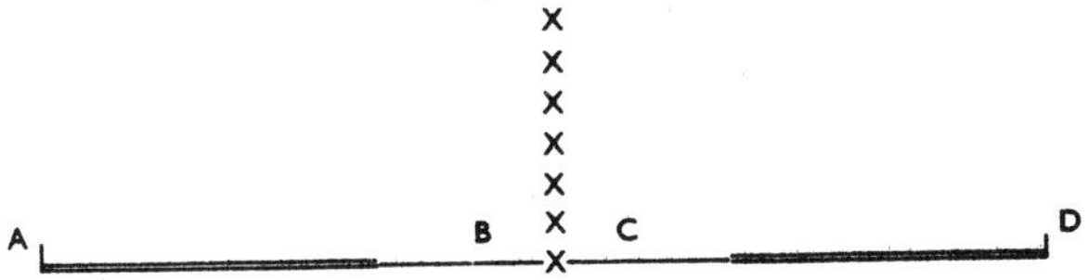

Passover: cross-section of set-up.

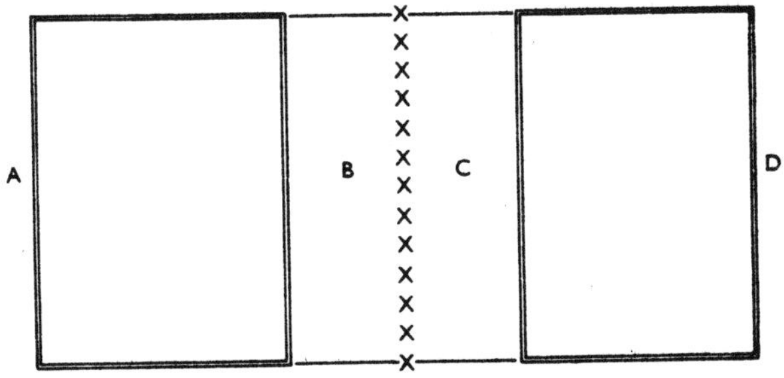

Passover: ground-plan of set-up.

Materials

- ☐ 1 × 1.70m (6ft) plank
- ☐ 1 × 125-litre (25-gall.) container
- ☐ 1 × 30m (100ft) rope
- ☐ 1 × bucket of water
- ☐ notebook and pen/pencil
- ☐ safety helmet for each group member
- ☐ gardening gloves for each member.

Time 40 minutes.

Safety

- Tutors' rulings on safety matters are final and binding.
- No one may jump from a height greater than one metre.
- Helmets and gloves must be worn.
- You must remain conscious of the need for safe working practices at all times.

GROUP 2 NOTES

Passover

Task The whole group and a bucket of water travel from area D to area A without the group, the bucket or the equipment touching the ground between D and C or B and A, and without either yourselves, the bucket, or your equipment touching the fence. You and your equipment *may* touch the ground between C and B. The penalty for breaking the rules is for the whole team, the bucket, and the equipment to return to the start.

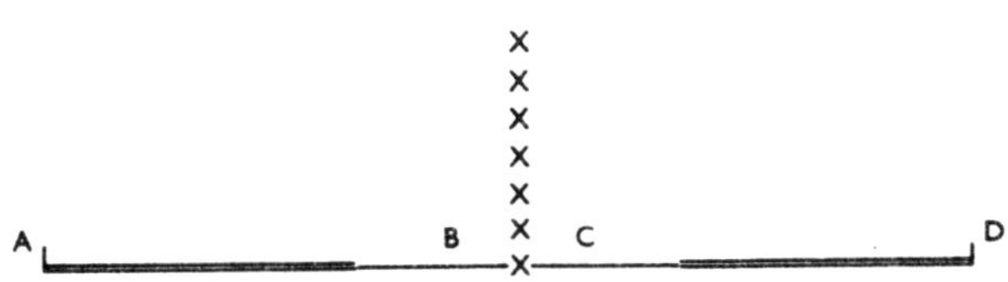

Passover: cross-section of set-up.

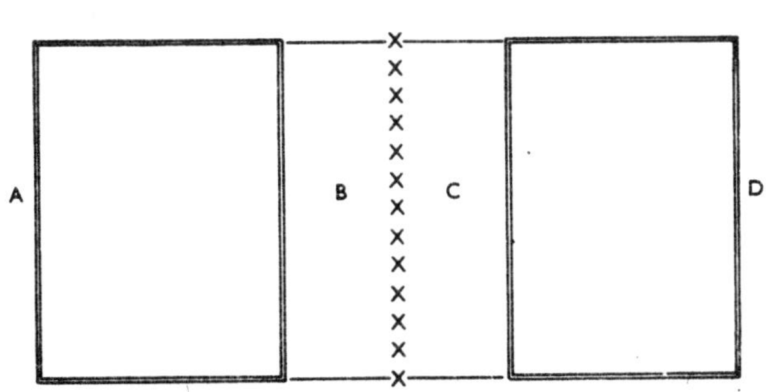

Passover: ground-plan of set-up.

Materials

- ☐ 1 × 1.70m (6ft) plank
- ☐ 1 × 125-litre (25-gall.) container
- ☐ 1 × 1.70m (6ft) ladder
- ☐ 1 × 30m (100ft) rope
- ☐ 1 × bucket of water
- ☐ notebook and pen/pencil
- ☐ climbing helmet for each group member
- ☐ gardening gloves for each member.

Time 40 minutes.

Safety

- Tutors' rulings on safety matters are final and binding.
- No one may jump from a height greater than one metre.
- Helmets and gloves must be worn.

16. THE CRATE ESCAPE

Facilitator notes

The Crate Escape is an exercise that demands planning, co-ordination, a good problem-solving process and adaptability. The task involves the group crossing a gap on 'stepping stones', which are positioned in such a way that several different methods are required.

Numbers 6 to 10.

Time Allow 30–40 minutes.

Materials

To set up the task

- ☐ site tape or similar to mark boundaries
- ☐ 6 × milk or beer crates

For group use

- ☐ 2 × 1.70m (6ft) planks
- ☐ 1 × 9m (30ft) rope
- ☐ safety helmets for each group member
- ☐ gloves for each group member.

Set-up

1. Mark start and finish lines, approximately 25m apart.
2. Place the crates in the pattern indicated on the set-up diagram, or your designed variation.
3. Crates can be made more secure with tent pegs or similar.
4. Place the group equipment behind the start line.

Procedure Having laid out the task, take the group to the start point and brief either the group or the leader.

Variations

- Increase the distance and number of crates.
- Require the team to take something with them (e.g. a bucket of water).
- Two teams start at opposite sides.

Safety

- Ensure that group members are careful when handling the planks, and that they wear helmets and gloves.
- Cover people who are jumping. It is advisable to discourage or even forbid anything over a couple of feet, as crates move easily.

Set-up diagram for Crate Escape

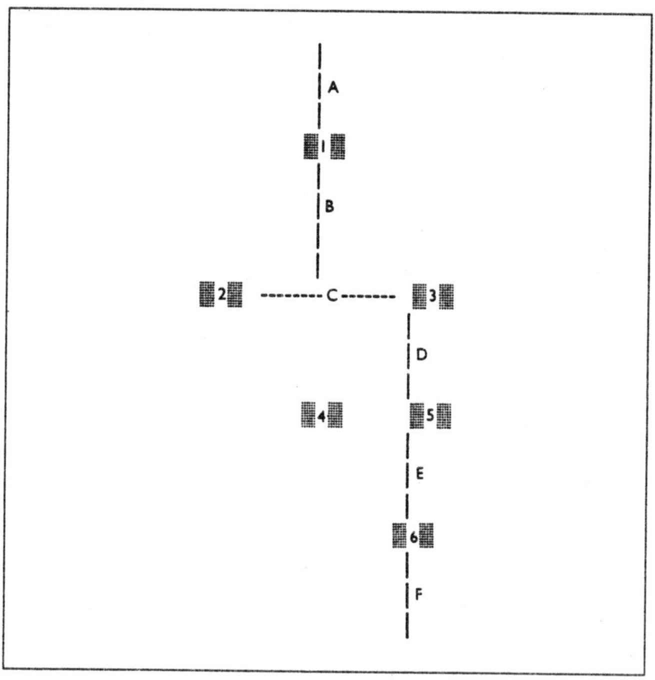

6 = crate

A = 1.6m or 5.5ft D = 1.6m or 5.5ft
B = 1.6m or 5.5ft E = 2.7m or 9.0ft
C = 1.6m or 5.5ft F = 1.6m or 5.5ft

- All distances are approximate, but single planks must not span the distance between crates 1 and 2, 1 and 3, or 5 and 6. It will be necessary to use 2 planks for each of these gaps.
- Between 1, 2 and 3 the planks must form a 'T'.
- Between 5 and 6 the planks need to be cantilevered.

GROUP NOTES

The crate escape

Objective To practise problem solving and teamwork.

Task The task is for your entire team to move from behind the start line to behind the finish line. Nobody and no equipment is to touch the ground between the tapes. If anyone or anything does, the whole team must start again. You must wear helmets and gloves. You may not move the 'stepping stones'.

Time 30 minutes.

Resources

- ☐ 2 × 1.70m (6ft) planks
- ☐ 1 × 9m (30ft) rope
- ☐ helmets for each group member
- ☐ gloves for each group member.

17. Triple barrel

Facilitator notes

Triple Barrel is an exercise with roots back in the days of the War Office Selection Board, and one with a clear and visible objective: for the group to travel from area A to area B (see diagram) using only the equipment provided, of which only the barrels may touch the ground in the marked area.

Numbers 4 to 6.

Time Allow 20 minutes.

Materials

To set up the task

- ☐ string/site tape for boundaries
- ☐ tent pegs/nails for securing boundaries.

For group use

- ☐ 3 × 225-litre (45-gall.) drums
- ☐ 2 × 2m (7ft) wooden planks
- ☐ safety helmets for each group member
- ☐ gardening gloves for each group member.

Procedure Having set up the exercise, take the group to a position around point A, where their equipment should be awaiting them, and give either the group or the leader the brief, allowing a few minutes for the group to digest the brief. Answer any amplifying questions but push back to the group any questions seeking clues as to how to do the task. After three minutes or so, announce that the task has started and it's over to them.

Review after the given time or when the group has completed the task, whichever is the sooner.

Prior training No prior training is required for this task, but an input on the necessity for safety wear and safe working is useful.

Safety

- Ensure that barrels are stable.
- Ensure that all group members are wearing helmets and gloves.
- Take care when delegates are counterbalancing, and intervene before anyone steps on one end of a plank which is not securely anchored – or before someone steps off, thus depriving others of a secure anchor.
- When the group reach side B, do not allow them to jump off. Instead, ensure that they step off. Help the first one off.

GROUP NOTES

Triple barrel

Task The whole group is to travel from area A to area B with only the drums touching the ground. The penalty for breaking the rules is that the whole group and its equipment return to the start.

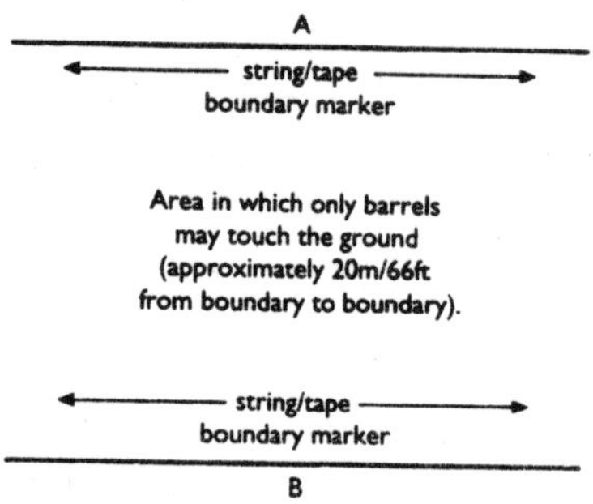

Materials

- ☐ 3 × 225-litre (45-gall.) drums
- ☐ 2 × 2m (7ft) wooden planks
- ☐ safety helmets for each group member
- ☐ gardening gloves for each group member.

You may not supplement this equipment.

Time 20 minutes.

Safety

- Tutors' rulings on matters of safety are final and binding.
- No one may jump from any structure you build.
- Helmets and gloves will be worn.
- You must be aware of the need for safe working practices at all times.

18. Twin Peaks

Facilitator notes

Twin Peaks is a teamwork and problem-solving exercise, requiring the team to cross a gap by means of barrels and a tyre. With only limited resources and a requirement for some physical prowess, it is essential that the team is aware of and makes best use of their human resources. People need to help each other physically, at least by holding hands.

Numbers 4 to 8.

Time Allow 20–30 minutes.

Materials

To set up the task

- ☐ 1 × convenient tree with accessible horizontal branch
- ☐ 2 × 45-gall. oil drums containing ballast
- ☐ 1 × tyre
- ☐ rope
- ☐ string or tape.

For group use

- ☐ 1 × 1.70m (6ft) plank
- ☐ 1 × 1.70m (6ft) rope
- ☐ safety helmet for each group member
- ☐ gloves for each group member.

Set-up

1. Suspend the tyre from the tree branch with the rope, so that the bottom of the tyre is approximately 1m from the ground.
2. Place the ballasted drums approximately 1.5m from the tyre on either side.
3. Mark start and finishing lines 1.4m from the drums. (The plank should reach from the ground behind the tape to the top of the barrel.)

Procedure Having laid out the task, take the group to a start point and brief either the group or the leader.

Safety Watch for carelessness with the plank and stay close to the tyre or the drums, if people are swinging, to prevent falls; but avoid assisting unnecessarily.

GROUP NOTES

Twin peaks

Your task is to get from A to B, as indicated by the tutor. Neither you nor any of your equipment may touch the ground or the tree.

Materials

- ☐ 1 × 1.70m (6ft) plank
- ☐ 1 × 1.70m (6ft) rope
- ☐ helmets
- ☐ gloves.

Time 20 minutes.

Safety

- Observe safe working practices. Your tutor will veto anything s/he considers dangerous.

19. Two short planks

Facilitator notes

Two Short Planks is a short, simple exercise with a number of solutions. It is ideal as a warm-up or teamwork exercise, particularly if you want people to help each other physically. Most solutions demand some holding of hands (or more!).

Numbers 4 to 8. (Higher numbers can be accommodated by forming teams to attempt the task in parallel, possibly in competition.)

Time Allow 20–30 minutes.

Materials

To set up the task

☐ site tape or similar to mark boundaries.

For group use

☐ 2 × 1.70 (6ft) planks
☐ 4 × 1.70 (6ft) ropes
☐ gloves for each group member.

Planks should ideally be just long enough for a complete team to stand on the two planks when laid parallel to each other.

Set-up Mark a start and finish line, approximately 15m apart. Place the group's equipment behind the start line.

Procedure Having laid out the task, take the group(s) to the start point and brief either the group or the leader. This task can benefit from a purely verbal brief, but be sure to get the instructions right. Throughout the exercise, watch for infringements, such as touching the ground to lift planks.

Safety Ensure that group members are careful when handling the planks and wear gloves to protect hands from splinters.

GROUP NOTES

Two short planks

The task is for your entire team to move from behind the start line to behind the finish line and back again, using only the equipment provided. Nobody is to touch the ground between the tapes. If anyone does the whole team must start again. You have 20 minutes.

20. Wayward Flock

Facilitator notes

Wayward Flock is a communication exercise, designed to highlight the importance of clear communication and the benefits of careful preparation. It is also a lot of fun!

Numbers 4 to 8.

Time Allow 30–40 minutes.

Materials

To set up the task

- ☐ 6 × short poles or canes, approx 1m high
- ☐ string or tape.

For group use

- ☐ a whistle (optional)
- ☐ blindfolds for all group members except one.

Set-up With the poles and string construct a pen large enough to hold the group, with an opening at one side just large enough to admit the largest delegate.

Procedure Having laid out the task, take the group to a start point and brief either the group or the leader. This task can benefit from a purely verbal brief, but be sure to get the instructions right. After the planning period, take the blindfolded 'sheep' and distribute them around the exercise area. It is best to have participants put on blindfolds before you place them.

Safety Stay close to any blindfolded group member when they move, watching for obstacles, but try to do it unobtrusively so as to maintain the balance between safety and an appropriate level of uncertainty, and so maximize the learning.

GROUP NOTES

Wayward flock

Objective To devise an effective system of communication.

Task The shepherd is to direct the sheep into the sheep pen. In 15 minutes' time all the sheep will be blindfolded and distributed around the immediate area, within the shepherd's view, by which time the group must have established a system of communication between shepherd and sheep.

Constraints

- Only the shepherd will be sighted; the rest – the sheep – will be blindfolded.
- The shepherd will be in a fixed spot 20 metres from the sheep pen, as directed by the tutor.
- No talking during the action phase.

Time 15 minutes' planning time. 20 minutes' execution time.

Resources

- ☐ your initiative
- ☐ 1 × whistle.

CHAPTER 7

NAVIGATION EXERCISES

21. A GOOD RUN FOR YOUR MONEY

Facilitator notes

This can be a simple task to set up, and brief, but requires some careful planning and organization by the groups to achieve the best result.

For the facilitator, in many locations, it can be conducted with a minimum of preparation, making use of permanent orienteering courses laid by local clubs, councils or other bodies. To use such sites you will be asked either to pay a fee or, more likely, to buy a printed map. For many such courses you can also buy the answers.

If no such splendid resource is available, you can prepare and lay out your own course, subject to suitable landowners' permission being obtained. This is time-consuming, but may be worthwhile if you are likely to use the same location and exercise on a number of occasions. You can prepare and run an orienteering exercise quite adequately from Ordnance Survey maps, although orienteering maps tend to be more detailed and of larger scale.

Orienteering or wayfaring is a sport which involves navigating from point to point using a detailed map, usually in complex terrain. The locations are marked on the map and described on a separate list. At the location there will typically be a post with a control code marked on it. There are often several courses in one area, of varying difficulty. It is this diversity that lends itself so well to our exercise. Whether you use an established course or your own, you will need to allocate points to locations. Ideally, the farther away and/or more difficult to reach a control point is, the greater its value.

The sample exercise quoted is based on Ilkley Moor in West Yorkshire and uses the courses prepared by Bradford Metropolitan District's Countryside Service and Airienteers (the orienteering club for Leeds, Bradford and the Yorkshire Dales.) Maps are available locally for a small fee. Similar courses exist in the Lake District, Wales and various other locations.

The task itself requires the teams to visit locations and note the control codes, which earn points. It can be run for one team or several, as a competition, as part of a larger exercise or to encourage co-operation.

Numbers Team(s) of 4 to 8.

Time Allow 60–120 minutes.

Materials

- ☐ orienteering maps
- ☐ lists of control points
- ☐ Ordnance Survey maps (optional)
- ☐ compasses (optional)
- ☐ romers or protractors

Set-up As stated above, this depends on the availability of prepared courses and maps, but in the best scenario there will be no set-up, except for allocating points to locations.

Procedure Sort out teams; remind everyone of the country code and safety rules; and brief either the groups or the leaders.

Prior training Short lessons in map reading, taking bearings and using romers may be appropriate. Ensure everyone, including experienced map readers, is aware of the different and additional symbols used on orienteering maps.

Alternatives Separate planning period.

Safety Ensure that people work at least in pairs and, if travelling any distance off road, in threes.

GROUP NOTES

A good run for your money

Objective To score as many points as possible in the time allowed.

Task To collect control numbers from various places around ________

Scoring Points will be awarded for correct control numbers on the team score card, according to the scale detailed.
Bonus points can be earned for early completion, 25 per minute for handing in score cards and 20 per minute for return of the complete team to base.
Penalty points will be incurred at 100 points per incorrect answer, and 50 points per minute per team member returning late.

Rules

- Maps must not be marked.
- You must travel at least in pairs away from the hotel, and in threes if going more than 500m from the road.
- Please obey the law and the country code.

Equipment

- ☐ maps
- ☐ compasses
- ☐ boots
- ☐ waterproofs
- ☐ yourselves!

Time You have one hour by the facilitator's watch.

TEAM SCORE CARD

Post	Number	Points	Post	Number	Points

Scoring detail

Ilkley Moor

Posts	*Points*
I, J	10
B, C, D, K, M, N, X	20
A, E, L, O, P, S, V	30
H, Q, U, W, Y	40
G, R, T, Z	50

Post locations

A Re-entrant (small valley)
B Hilltop
C Boulder, east side
D Between the knolls
E Foot of steep slope
F Gully bend
G North-eastern re-entrant
H Boulder, north-eastern side
I Marsh, south end
J Tarn edge
K Rocky ridge, north end
L Marsh, south-eastern edge
M Depression
N Marsh, south edge
O Ditch end
P Tarn, west end
Q Hilltop
R Re-entrant
S Gully
T Boulder, north side
U Knoll, south-eastern foot
V Steep slope, foot
W Gully
X Thicket, East side
Y Southern gully
Z Boulder, south side

22. Black box

Facilitator notes

Black Box is a versatile and exacting exercise. The scenario is a simple search operation, requiring minimal set-up and preparation by the facilitator, but which demands a high level of organization, planning and co-ordination by the participants.

The exercise lends itself to many areas and types of terrain. Typically run in open country, as in the example quoted, it can easily be run in a park or even on a housing estate. If run even in part on private land, be sure to seek and obtain access permission, or place the relevant areas out of bounds.

Numbers 8 upwards.

Time 2–3 hours.

Materials

To set up the task

- ☐ a Black Box. Almost anything will do, but an old ammunition box, available from Army surplus stores, is ideal. It can be painted or covered for greater authenticity. A 'Please Do Not Disturb' sign is a sensible precaution, and a contact telephone number is also appropriate.

For group use

- ☐ maps
- ☐ compasses

- ☐ torches
- ☐ whistles
- ☐ grid referencing aids (e.g. Silva romer)
- ☐ suitable footwear and clothing.

Set-up Obtain landowners' permission; position the Black Box in an appropriate place.

Procedure Brief the group or leader. Allow time for absorption and answer any amplifying questions whilst deflecting any questions seeking ways to achieve the task. Once the questions have been dealt with, announce that the time has started and it's over to them. Review after the allowed time has elapsed or after the group has completed the task, whichever is the sooner.

Prior training Short lessons in map reading, taking bearings and using romers may be appropriate.

Safety A full safety brief should be given, appropriate to the terrain. Ensure people work in at least pairs or threes.

GROUP NOTES

Black Box

Background An aircraft has crashed at Grid Reference ________ . The aircraft wreckage has been removed, but the 'Black Box' with in-flight information is missing. The accident research team are confident it is somewhere within the confines of the old perimeter fence (marked on your master map). The box is metal, black with red-and-white stripes.

Task Your task is to find and recover the Black Box.

Constraints

- You may not operate outside the perimeter fence.
- You must not enter any buildings.
- ______________ is outside the search area, and must not be entered.
- You must operate in at least twos/threes throughout the exercise.
- You must establish and staff a central control point, where all sub-teams' locations must be recorded.
- No vehicles may be used.

Time You have two and a half hours, including planning and travelling time. All team members must be back at the start point by the end of that time.

Resources

- ☐ maps
- ☐ compasses
- ☐ whistles
- ☐ torches
- ☐ grid referencing aids
- ☐ transport to and from the search area.

23. Cakes and Ale

Facilitator notes

Cakes and Ale is a task in which two groups navigate around an area of countryside in search of clues which lead them to opposite sides of a stretch of water, where they exchange goods by means of a system which they build themselves. The exercise is supported by an elaborate brief which gives a rationale for their doing this.

In the first (clue-searching) phase, groups are free to choose whether or not they compete or co-operate. In the second (goods-exchanging) phase, competition is not an option; to succeed they must co-operate.

Numbers 10 to 16 (preferably equal numbers per team).

Time Allow 150 minutes.

Materials

For set up

- ☐ *Appropriate map:* we recommend the relevant 1:25,000 Ordnance Survey *Pathfinder* or *Outdoor Leisure* maps.
- ☐ 4 × 2.3m (8ft) poles, approximately 10cm (4in.) in diameter
- ☐ 10 × 2.3m (8ft) rope for lashings, etc.
- ☐ 3 × 30m (100ft) 8mm polypropylene ropes
- ☐ 1 × pulley wheel (with attachment point)
- ☐ a cake for every member of both groups (alternatively, one very large cake and a knife)

- ☐ a can/bottle of ale for every member of both groups (or appropriate soft drinks for non-drinkers)
- ☐ a plastic washing basket or similar container.

For group use (per group)

- ☐ *3 copies of the appropriate map.* If the exercise is to be used frequently, we suggest that the relevant area and its immediate surroundings be cut from the map and laminated, or covered with clear plastic sheet and attached to clipboards
- ☐ pencils or (in the case of laminated maps or those covered with clear plastic sheeting) water-soluble overhead-projector pens or Chinagraph pencils
- ☐ a small notebook for each delegate
- ☐ a passenger vehicle and driver for each group
- ☐ 6 × grid-referencing aids (e.g. Silva romer).

Procedure Having set up the exercise, divide the group into two teams, take each team to separate rooms and brief the teams or the leaders, allowing them a few minutes to ask any appropriate amplifying questions. Push back to the teams any questions seeking clues as to how to do the task. After questions, announce the time has started, and it's over to them.

Prior training The ability to read a map and use a grid referencing aid to establish 8-figure grid references is vital to this task. If the delegates do not already possess these skills, training for at least 2 per team is necessary. (See pages 278–284.)

Safety

- Resist the temptation to allow group members to drive. There are few greater hazards than a delegate in pursuit of a deadline.
- Although the exercise only requires minimal walking, always be sure that you know when delegates are walking, their destination, and their estimated time of return. Insist that they walk in pairs at the very least, and stay within sight and sound of one another. If they are to go on foot in wild country, they should go in threes.
- If the exchange is to take place at water of any depth (1m or more), apply safety precautions for water-based exercises.

Set-up Although the exercise takes some time to prepare in a new location, once it has been prepared it can be used repeatedly.

Mark two sets of clue sites and the exchange site on your master map. Clue sites for each group should be spread across a wide area (approximately a 12km square), but clues for each team should be close to the corresponding clue for the other team (see diagram below).

Most of the clues should be by the roadside, and at such places as road junctions, which are easily found on a map and have useful items of street furniture (signposts etc.) at which to place clues.

It is likely that you will have to drive around the terrain in question to establish the best sites. This will also give you a 'feel' for the distances involved.

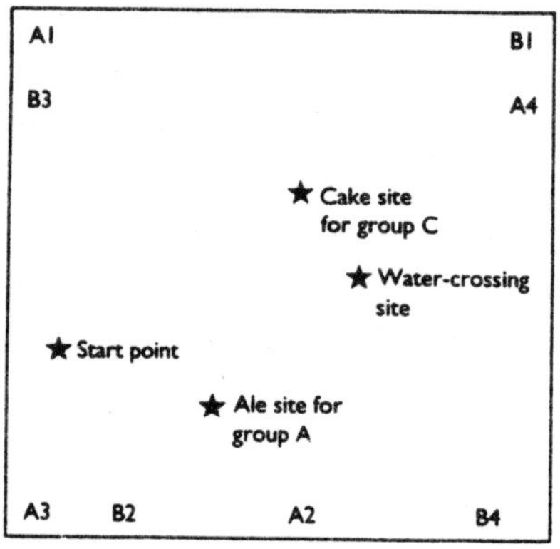

A typical layout of sites (not to scale).

Having identified the sites, write a message giving the location of the cakes or ale (depending on the group) and the exchange-site, cut these messages into four quarters each, bag them up and deposit them at sites A1 to A4 for the 'Ale' group and sites C1 to C4 for the 'Cake' group. On the group notes fill in the start information with grid references and descriptions of the appropriate four sites for each group.

Shortly before the exercise commences, put the cakes, ale, and river-crossing equipment at their respective sites. River-crossing equipment should be divided thus:

'Cake' side of water

☐ 4 × 2.3m (8ft) poles, approximately 10cm (4in.) in diameter

☐ 1 × 30m (100ft) 8mm polypropylene ropes
☐ 1 × plastic washing basket or similar container.

'Ale' side of water

☐ 10 × 2.3m (8ft) lengths of rope for lashings, etc.
☐ 2 × 30m (100ft) 8mm polypropylene ropes
☐ 1 × pulley wheel (with attachment point).

Ensure that you make a note on the master map or a separate list of which articles have gone where. Messages should be placed less than 24 hours before the exercise and should bear a note to the effect that they are part of a training exercise and will be cleared away within 48 hours.

Issue the groups with maps, romers, the relevant group brief, pens and notepads.

Group 'A'

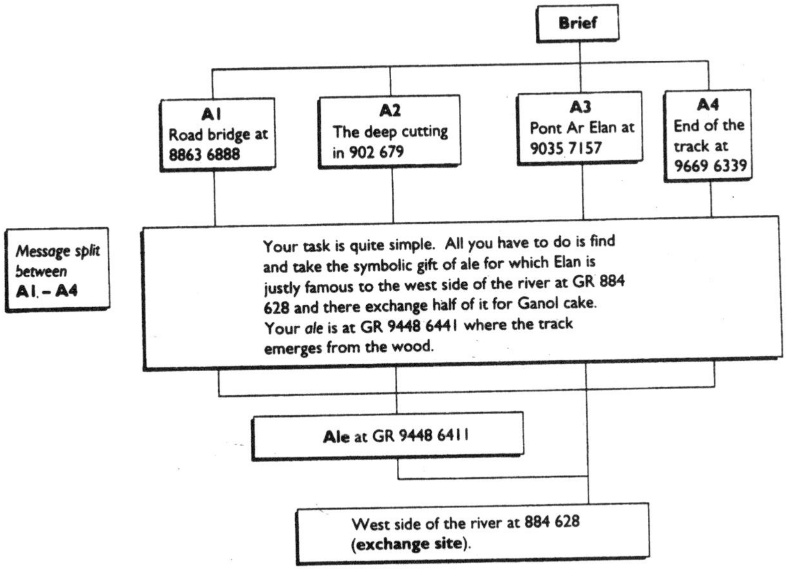

Information flowchart for Cakes and Ale exercise based around Elan Village, Rhayader, Powys (Group A).

Group 'C'

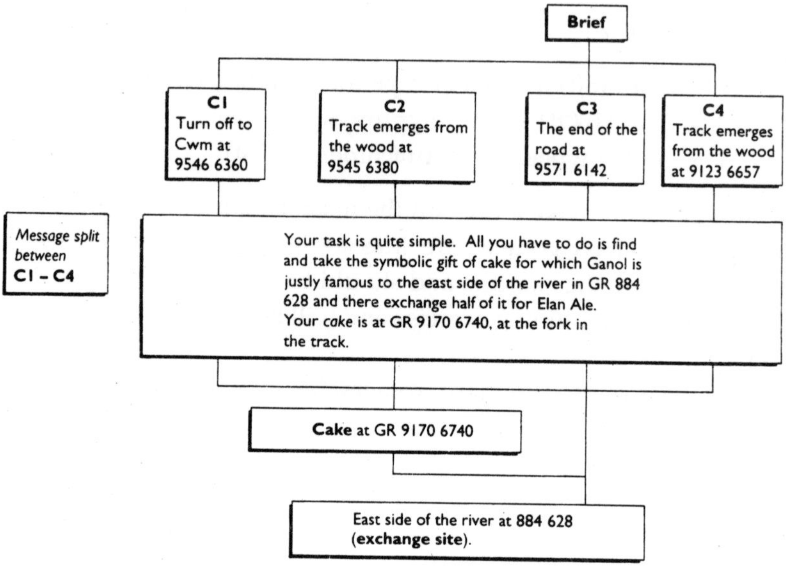

Information flowchart for Cakes and Ale Exercise based around Elan Village, Rhayader, Powys (Group C).

GROUP NOTES

Cakes and ale

The Task The neighbouring ancient parishes of ________________ and ______________________ have always been rivals, chronically unable to co-operate with each other on the simplest of matters.

The Councils of both parishes are aware that this state of affairs isn't helpful to anyone and is particularly damaging to development of the area. Anxious to build up a more friendly spirit, Councillors have suggested an annual event called the 'Cakes and Ale Gala', which, it is hoped, will replace the current event in which local youths annually hurl insults and old fruit at each other.

The event *must* be successful if communal relationships are to be improved. Your task is to 'product-test' the event.

You represent __________ The other group represents __________ The organizers have left the following message, which should help you to get started. The message is:

1. ____

2. ____

3. ____

4. ____

Transport Each team manages one vehicle and driver. The driver will obey the law, and will not navigate.

Equipment provided for your team is as follows:

- ☐ 3 copies of the appropriate map
- ☐ pencils or map marking pens. Please do not use anything else to mark the maps
- ☐ a small notebook for each of you
- ☐ 6 × grid-referencing aids.

Time The maximum time allowed for this exercise is 150 minutes.

Safety

- On no account should you drive your own or each other's vehicles.
- Always tell a member of course staff your destination and estimated journey time if you have to walk any distance. If leaving the building or one of the vehicles on foot, you must stay in groups of two or more – three in wild country.
- Other rules may be introduced, depending on conditions at the time.

24. Cook's tour

Facilitator notes

Cook's tour is a simple exercise, which requires considerable preparation for the first time you run it, but thereafter virtually none. The task requires the team to visit a number of locations and collect the answers to a series of questions. It can be run for one team or several, as a competition, as part of a larger exercise, or to encourage co-operation.

Numbers Team(s) of 4 to 8.

Time Allow 60–90 minutes.

Materials

- ☐ Ordnance Survey maps (1 per two participants)
- ☐ compasses (optional)
- ☐ romers or protractors.

Set-up If utilizing an area for the first time, devise your own question list, and keep a record of the answers. Beware of clues that may be moved or changed, such as bus times, etc. If used, such clues may need checking each time the exercise is run. For this reason, a sample set of questions for Ripon, North Yorkshire is included, but not the answers!

Procedure Sort out teams; remind everyone of country code and safety rules, and brief either the groups or the leaders.

Prior training Short lessons in map reading, taking bearings and using romers may be appropriate. (See pages 278–284.)

Alternatives Separate planning period; provide some transport, such as bicycles or motor vehicles, acting as taxis.

Safety Ensure that the group reads and understands the appropriate safety notes. (See pages 48–49.)

GROUP NOTES

Cook's tour

Task You are to earn as many points as possible in the time allocated by visiting the locations below and correctly answering the corresponding question. Correct answers earn the score indicated. The same score is *deducted* for wrong answers. If a question is not attempted, there is no charge either way. All answers must be submitted together.

Points scored may be increased at the following rates:

0–30	points	no bonus
31–40	points	10 bonus points
41–60	points	20 bonus points
61–70	points	50 bonus points
71–80	points	100 bonus points
81–90	points	500 bonus points
91–100	points	1000 bonus points.

If over 50 points are earned with no wrong answers there will be a further bonus of 1000.

Constraints

- You must operate in at least pairs at all times.
- You must operate in threes when walking more than 500m from recognized roads.
- You must abide by the country code.
- No transport is to be used.
- Avoid disturbing the public and do not telephone them for answers!

Time You have 90 minutes.

1. What time is evensong at St. Mary's Chapel, Ripon? 3 pts.
2. What now happens at Ripon Railway Station? 5 pts.
3. What is the highest mileage on the signpost at GR 3232 7338? 8 pts.
4. To where does the signpost at GR 330730 direct you? 4 pts.
5. In the pub at Sharow, what aircraft is pictured on the wall? 5 pts.
6. What initials are on the yellow sign at GR 3185 7207? 1 pt.
7. What metal structure is in the wall at GR 330717? 5 pts.
8. At GR 306730 what can not get through? 4 pts.
9. When would you go to the clinic at GR 316709 for chiropody? 2 pts.
10. What date appears over 29 and 30 High St. Agnes Gate? 3 pts.
11. What telephone number is displayed in the Crypt at Ripon Cathedral? 5 pts.
12. On what is the name 'Rough House' mounted at GR 267679? 5 pts.
13. What does the Mayor do next to the ladies' toilet in Ripon Market Place? 1 pt.
14. In the Valley of Seven Bridges, between Fountains Abbey and Ripon, what are the bridges made of? 10 pts.
15. What is kept alive by Robert and Elizabeth's tomb in the churchyard at Aldfield? 6 pts.
16. What is the 'name' of the footpath at GR 291715? 4 pts.
17. What is the score at Ripon Cricket Club? 3 pts.
18. Draw a diagram of Lacon Cross, GR 244666. 10 pts.
19. What mythical animals guard the lake outlet at GR 282692? 7 pts.
20. How many clock faces are on the tower at the road junction at GR 306709? 5 pts.

25. The rescuers

Facilitator notes

This 'mountain-rescue' activity is challenging, exciting and demanding. As with all such activities, it is important to provide a role for those less fit or able than others, such as the supporting role detailed below. It is not necessary to pretend the rescue is real to get the learning from the exercise; indeed, if not wholly convincing such pretence can detract from the exercise.

Numbers 8 to 20.

Time 1–2 hours.

Materials

For the casualty

- ☐ sleeping-bag
- ☐ survival bag
- ☐ flask of hot drink.

For the group

- ☐ climbing helmets
- ☐ maps
- ☐ compasses
- ☐ rucksacks
- ☐ whistles
- ☐ torches
- ☐ suitable clothing

- ☐ walkie-talkies (optional)
- ☐ first aid kit
- ☐ stretcher
- ☐ rope
- ☐ tea-making facilities (not flasks).

Set-up A 'casualty' needs to be briefed and pre-positioned in the area, within a reasonable distance from the walkers' expected route. This should be someone well qualified, competent and equipped to go out alone; if not, they should be escorted.

Procedure This task benefits from a verbal brief, adding immediacy and realism to the scenario. The brief may be supplemented by a number of grid references the walkers are expected to visit, a route card, or a limited area to search.

Safety Normal safety rules apply, including staff ratios. Take particular care when the victim is being moved.

GROUP NOTES

The rescuers

A walker has just been reported overdue from a walk in the __________ area. The local fell rescue team are already involved at another incident and you have been asked to assist. The walker is understood to be experienced and well equipped. A copy of their intended route is available.

You are to find the missing walker and, if possible bring him/her back to the nearest road. You are to leave a sub-team at the roadside to coordinate your search, liaise with the fell rescue team on arrival, and prepare a hot drink for the victim and rescue party.

Equipment

- ☐ helmets
- ☐ maps
- ☐ rucksacks
- ☐ compasses
- ☐ whistles
- ☐ rope
- ☐ torches
- ☐ suitable clothing
- ☐ walkie-talkies
- ☐ first aid kit
- ☐ stretcher
- ☐ tea-making facilities.

You must operate in groups of at least three at all times. Safety rules must be strictly observed.

26. Riotous assembly

Facilitator notes

Riotous Assembly is a task in which two groups compete or co-operate to assemble plastic models (usually aeroplanes) for cash. Parts of the model are acquired by visiting sites at which codewords and information leading to further sites (and thus further codewords) have been placed. The brief is silent on the matter of co-operation versus competition, which is thus a matter for the groups to decide.

Income is earned against a time-completion matrix so that the longer the groups take, the less they earn. A further element of decision-making is provided by the fact that groups can cash-in at any time after the first 55 minutes.

Numbers 10 to 18 (split into two teams). Equal numbers per team are desirable, but not necessary.

Time 135 minutes.

Materials

For set-up

- ☐ *appropriate map.* We recommend the relevant 1:25,000 scale Ordnance Survey *Pathfinder* or *Outdoor Leisure* maps, but have also used (in cities) *A to Z*, *Geographia*, or similar guides which have street names included, unlike most Ordnance Survey maps.
- ☐ a supply of visiting-card-sized blank cards
- ☐ a supply of 7in. × 9in. or similar plastic bags
- ☐ adhesive tape

- ☐ write-on labels
- ☐ 2 × unbuilt model aeroplanes per team
- ☐ polystyrene cement (2 tubes per team)
- ☐ 1 craft knife per team.

For group use (per group)

- ☐ *3 copies of the appropriate map.* If the exercise is to be used frequently, we suggest that the relevant area and its immediate surroundings be cut from the map (taking care to include or replace the grid numbers) and laminated, or covered with clear plastic sheet and attached to clipboards.
- ☐ pencils or (in the case of laminated maps or those covered with clear plastic sheeting) water-soluble overhead projector pens or Chinagraph pencils
- ☐ 6 × grid-referencing aids (e.g. the Silva romer)
- ☐ a small notebook for each delegate
- ☐ a vehicle and staff member as driver per team
- ☐ a mobile phone per vehicle (optional)
- ☐ access to a telephone at base.

Procedure Having set up the exercise, divide the group into two teams, take each team to a separate room and brief the teams or their leaders, allowing them a few minutes to ask any appropriate amplifying questions. Push back to the teams any questions seeking clues as to how to do the task. After questions, announce the time has started, and it's over to them.

Prior training The ability to read a map and use a grid-referencing aid to establish eight-figure grid references is vital to this task. If the delegates do not already possess these skills, training is necessary. This need not be for *all* delegates, but at least 2 per team should have the necessary skill. (See pages 278–284.)

Variations The exercise has a number of useful variations. These include:

- *the single-group option.* This is particularly useful for small groups.
- *the on-foot option.* The exercise can be set up as an on-foot task, with suitably shorter distances. See safety rules, pages 48–49.
- *the multi-team option.* With additional locations, the exercise can be

run with any number of groups. This adds a fascinating inter-team political scenario.

- *larger versions:* We have concentrated here on the 135-minute/16-location basic version of the exercise. On other occasions, we have successfully expanded the exercise to a maximum of 270 minutes with 26 locations.

Set-up Although the exercise takes some time to prepare in a new location, once it has been prepared it can be used repeatedly. It is prepared in the following way:

Mark two sets of clue sites on your master map. Clue sites for each group should be spread across a wide area (approximately a 12km square), but clues for each team should be close to the corresponding clue for the other group. It is also quite useful for clues to be split into 2 separate 'zones' to facilitate cost savings in travel (see diagrams).

The vast majority of clues should be at the roadside, and at such places as road junctions, which are easily found on a map and have useful items of street furniture (signposts etc.) at which to place clues. It is likely that you will have to drive around the terrain in question to establish the best sites. This will also give you a 'feel' for the distances involved.

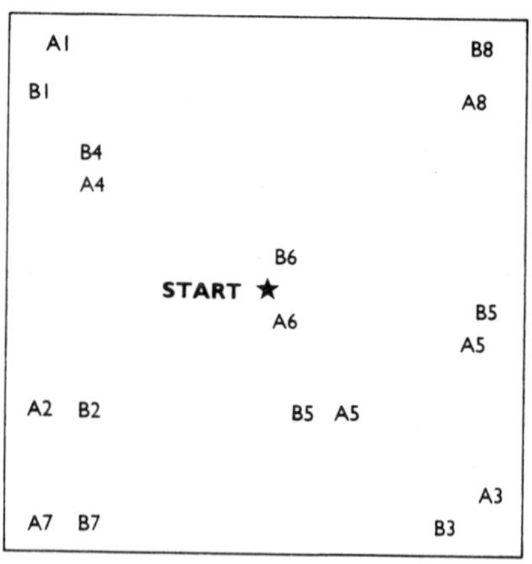

A typical layout of sites (not to scale).

Having identified the sites, write codewords of your own devising on the cards, add clues and part-clues to other locations (see diagram for a typical flow of clues), seal all in plastic bags (labelled for your own convenience) and place them at the sites in question, making a note on the master map or a separate list of which codewords have gone where. The purpose of codewords is to liberate bits of plastic models, glue, etc., to the central team which most groups will have set up.

Bag-up the models, polystyrene cement, etc., ensuring that groups will receive these in a roughly sequential order (i.e. adhesive and first bits early in the exercise, last bits late in the exercise).

Codewords, etc., should be placed less than 24 hours before the exercise and should bear a message to the effect that they are part of a training exercise and will be cleared away within 48 hours.

Issue the group maps together with romers, the group brief, pens and notepads.

After the exercise, pay any money owed and ensure that any clues which have not been collected by the group are cleared away.

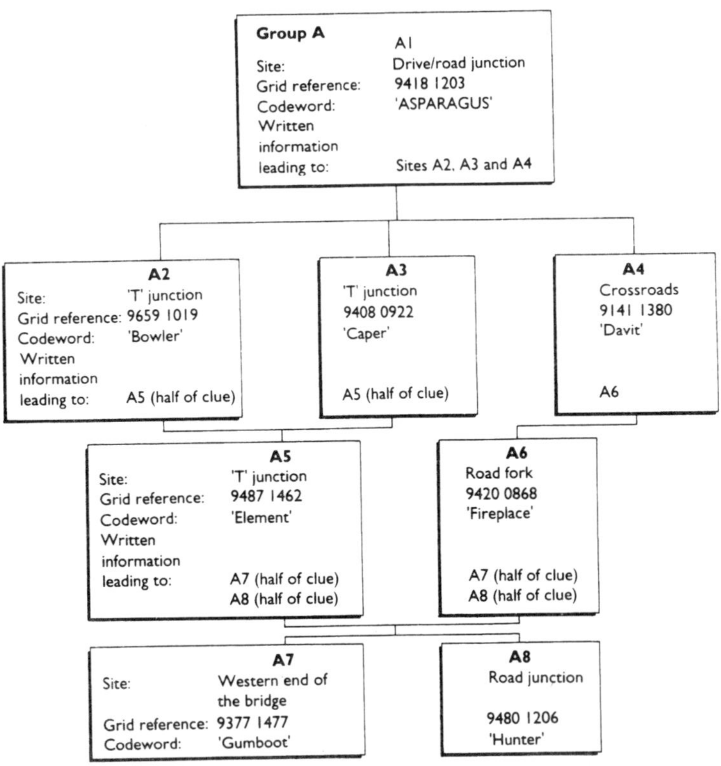

Information flowchart for Riotous Assembly exercise based around Tring, Herts. (Group A).

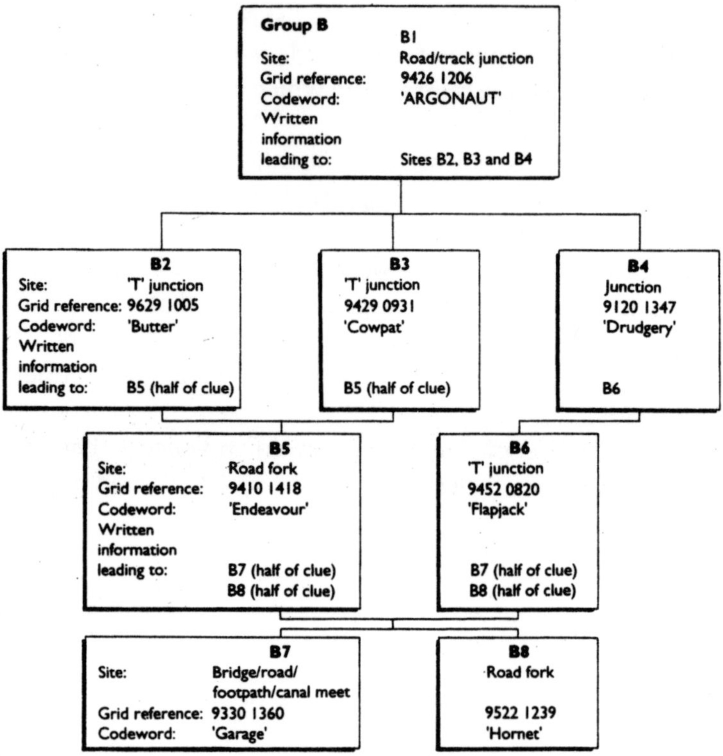

Information flowchart for Riotous Assembly exercise based around Tring, Herts. (Group B).

GROUP A NOTES

Riotous assembly

The task is to *retrieve* codewords which have been placed in and around this area, exchange the codewords for unassembled parts of a particular object, and *assemble* that object. 50% of your profits are made from retrieval, 50% from assembly, so both are equally important. Just like a real business, you stand to make profits or accrue losses, depending on your effectiveness as a team.

We have attached a financial reward/costs table. Note that in addition, a bonus of £3.00 is payable to the most successful team. In the event of a tie, this sum is divided equally between the two teams.

Transport Your team may use *one* vehicle, driven by a member of the course staff, who will act as obedient but law-abiding chauffeurs. You may not use other vehicles.

Penalties Anyone failing to be in their team room at closedown time will be fined at a rate of 50p per person per minute or part thereof.

Start information The first codeword awaits you at grid reference __________. Further information is also there.

Equipment provided for your team is as follows:

- ☐ 3 copies of the appropriate map. Please only mark these with pencil or, if plastic-covered, the pens provided.
- ☐ pencils or map-marking pens

- [ ] 6 grid-referencing aids
- [ ] a vehicle and staff member as driver
- [ ] a mobile phone per vehicle, number given on request from the driver.

Time 135 minutes maximum.

Safety rules See separate sheet attached.

Profit and loss Set out below is a table of profit and loss expressed in £ sterling. Make sure you understand its implications.

Time in minutes	*% of task completed*									
	10	20	30	40	50	60	70	80	90	100
<55	£1	£2	£3	£4	£5	£6	£7	£8	£9	£10
65	£0	£1	£2	£3	£4	£5	£6	£7	£8	£9
75	–£1	£0	£1	£2	£3	£4	£5	£6	£7	£8
85	–£2	–£1	£0	£1	£2	£3	£4	£5	£6	£7
95	–£3	–£2	–£1	£0	£1	£2	£3	£4	£5	£6
105	–£4	–£3	–£2	–£1	£0	£1	£2	£3	£4	£5
115	–£5	–£4	–£3	–£2	–£1	£0	£1	£2	£3	£4
125	–£6	–£5	–£4	–£3	–£2	–£1	£0	£1	£2	£3
135	–£7	–£6	–£5	–£4	–£3	–£2	–£1	£0	£1	£2

GROUP B NOTES

Riotous assembly

The task is to *retrieve* codewords which have been placed in and around this area, exchange the codewords for unassembled parts of a particular object, and *assemble* that object. 50% of your profits are made from retrieval, 50% from assembly, so both are equally important. Just like a real business, you stand to make profits or accrue losses, depending on your effectiveness as a team.

We have attached a financial reward/costs table. Note that in addition, a bonus of £3.00 is payable to the most successful team. In the event of a tie, this sum is divided equally between the two teams.

Transport Your team may use *one* vehicle, driven by a member of the course staff, who will act as obedient but law-abiding chauffeurs. You may not use other vehicles.

Penalties Anyone failing to be in their team room at closedown time will be fined at a rate of 50p per person per minute or part thereof.

Start information The first codeword awaits you at grid reference __________. Further information is also there.

Equipment provided for your team is as follows:

- ☐ 3 copies of the appropriate map. Please only mark these with pencil or, if plastic-covered, the pens provided.
- ☐ pencils or map-marking pens

- ☐ 6 grid-referencing aids
- ☐ a vehicle and staff member as driver
- ☐ a mobile phone per vehicle, number given on request from the driver.

Time 135 minutes maximum.

Safety rules See separate sheet attached.

Profit and loss Set out below is a table of profit and loss expressed in £ sterling. Make sure you understand its implications.

Time in minutes	*% of task completed*									
	10	20	30	40	50	60	70	80	90	100
<55	£1	£2	£3	£4	£5	£6	£7	£8	£9	£10
65	£0	£1	£2	£3	£4	£5	£6	£7	£8	£9
75	–£1	£0	£1	£2	£3	£4	£5	£6	£7	£8
85	–£2	–£1	£0	£1	£2	£3	£4	£5	£6	£7
95	–£3	–£2	–£1	£0	£1	£2	£3	£4	£5	£6
105	–£4	–£3	–£2	–£1	£0	£1	£2	£3	£4	£5
115	–£5	–£4	–£3	–£2	–£1	£0	£1	£2	£3	£4
125	–£6	–£5	–£4	–£3	–£2	–£1	£0	£1	£2	£3
135	–£7	–£6	–£5	–£4	–£3	–£2	–£1	£0	£1	£2

27. Round the Houses

Facilitator notes

Round the Houses is an exercise which combines elements of navigation with field exercises, thus having several dimensions.

Numbers Up to 4 teams of 4–6 members.

Time Allow 4–5 hours.

Materials

For navigation

- ☐ *2 copies per group of the appropriate map.* If the exercise is to be used frequently, we suggest that the relevant area and its immediate surroundings be cut from the map (taking care to include or replace the grid numbers) and laminated or covered with clear plastic sheet and attached to clipboards.
- ☐ pencils or (in the case of laminated maps or those covered with clear plastic sheeting) water-soluble overhead projector pens or Chinagraph pencils
- ☐ 6 × grid-referencing aids (e.g. the Silva romer) per group
- ☐ a small notebook for each delegate.

For field exercises

Equipment for the following exercises:

- ☐ *Container Ferry*
- ☐ *First Service*
- ☐ *Playing a Blinder*
- ☐ *Triple Barrel*

Procedure Having set up the task, take the teams to the various start-points and leave each with a staff member, who briefs the team or leader, answers amplifying questions, and then announces that the clock has started and it's over to them. Teams dropped earlier than others may have to wait until an agreed time in order to allow all teams to start at once.

Variations

- With a little imagination, even larger variants can be written.
- Cash or points elements can be added to make it a competition if so desired.
- We often give groups a'joker' to play (as in *Jeux Sans Frontières*), which adds a further element of decision.

Safety See notes for navigation exercises (page 49).

Set-up Although the exercise takes some time to prepare in a new location, once it has been prepared it can be used repeatedly.

1. Set up the exercises *Container Ferry, First Service, Playing a Blinder* and *Triple Barrel* at about equal points on an approximately 8km 'round trip' route. The course can be over public rights of way, roads, or a mixture of the two, although it is logistically useful to have the exercises as near to roads as possible.
2. Note the grid references of the exercise sites and write these (and the site numbers) on cards, which should be attached to the exercise briefs so that the site of the next exercise is given along with the exercise brief at each location.
3. Issue four of these sets to tutorial staff accompanying groups.
4. Drop the groups (equipped with maps, etc.), one at each exercise, and let tutors issue the briefs at a prearranged time.

Pre-set tasks should be placed only a few hours before the exercise and should bear a message to the effect that they are part of a training exercise and will be cleared away within 8 hours.

Ensure that the exercise is cleared quickly after final completion.

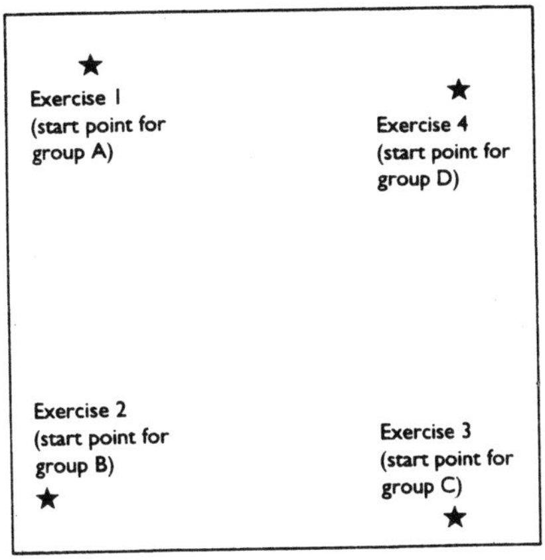

A typical layout of sites (not to scale). Groups move from exercise to exercise in clockwise fashion, so that there is only one group at any site at one time.

GROUP NOTES

Round the houses

Task Your group is to manage itself through a series of exercises to which you have to navigate on foot. _____ other groups are also doing the same task.

You are at the site of your first exercise. When requested, your tutor will give you the brief together with the location of the next exercise. Further locations will be revealed as you go along. There are 4 locations, roughly equally apart.

The exercise ends when you complete the fourth task. Transport will be provided from there back to base.

Points can be earned for each task, at a rate of 6 points for the best result, 5 for the second, and so on, down to 3 for the least effective performance. Failure to seriously attempt an exercise earns no points for that task.

Failure to be at the site of the last task within the allotted time incurs a fine of 1 point per person per 5 minutes late.

Equipment

- ☐ 2 maps of the relevant area
- ☐ pencils or map-marking pens
- ☐ 6 grid-referencing aids
- ☐ a small notebook each.

Time 4 hours.

Safety rules are attached.

28. Trails and Tribulations

Facilitator notes

Trails and Tribulations is a task in which a group navigates around an area of countryside in search of tokens which have been set out beforehand. The tokens have a cash value which is enhanced if full sets are gathered, much in the same way as the sets in *Monopoly* are worth more if one player owns them. The brief is set in a commercial scenario, and allows a clever group to minimize its physical efforts and make a good profit. There are strong financial penalties for late returns, and 3 or 4 people returning 10 minutes late can lead to the group sustaining a loss. We often use real money in this exercise, as even small sums add a great feeling of reality.

Numbers 10 to 15.

Time Allow 1 hour 45 minutes, plus time for travel to and from the start.

Equipment

For set-up

- ☐ *Appropriate map.* We recommend the relevant 1:25,000 scale Ordnance Survey *Pathfinder* or *Outdoor Leisure* maps, but have also used orienteering maps and even (in cities) *A to Z*, *Geographia*, or similar guides which have street names included, unlike most Ordnance Survey maps.
- ☐ a supply of visiting-card sized blank cards.

For group use

- ☐ *4 or 5 copies of the appropriate map* marked with the exercise sites. If the exercise is to be used frequently, we suggest that the relevant area and its immediate surroundings be cut from the map and laminated or covered with clear plastic sheet and attached to clipboards.
- ☐ pencils or (in the case of laminated maps or those covered with clear plastic sheeting) water-soluble overhead projector pens or Chinagraph pencils
- ☐ a small notebook for each delegate.

Procedure Having set up the exercise, take the group to the start position and brief either the group or the leader, allowing them to ask any appropriate amplifying questions. Push back to the group any questions seeking clues as to how to do the task. After questions, announce the time has started, and it's over to them.

Prior training Prior training or existing ability in mapwork (see pages 278–284) is very useful for this task.

Safety

- Beware of the level of physical stress to which groups can subject themselves, and do not allow them to be split into groups of less than 3. This means that if one group member has a mishap, there is someone to stay with them and someone else to fetch help. Although our experience over 10 years is accident-free, it is worth remembering that people can twist ankles in urban and lowland environments as well as in wild country.
- Clothing depends on the prevailing conditions. If any off-road work at all is involved, walking boots should be worn. Strongly discourage the wearing of waterproofs on dry days (especially hot ones), but provide small rucksacks in which to carry them.
- Always ensure that you have a record of the planned routes and estimated time of return for each group member.
- People can dehydrate easily. Provide drinks for them to carry in their rucksacks. *Do not under any circumstances* provide alcohol – this dehydrates people.
- During the active phase of the exercise, patrol the routes and try to keep tabs on each sub-group.

- The exercise is not recommended for those who suffer from heart, respiratory, or similar difficulties.

Set-up Although the exercise takes some time to prepare in a new location, once it has been prepared it can be used repeatedly with minimal time and effort.

Mark 4 sets of clue sites on your master map. These sets should be mingled together (see diagram below) and should be graded by difficulty of access. In effect, clues in class D should be easy to find, in class C slightly less accessible, and so on, through to class A, which should be quite difficult to find.

It is likely that you will have to walk the ground in question to establish exactly which sites are easy to locate, and which are more obscure. This will also give you a 'feel' for the distances involved. The ideal set-up is one in which, if groups choose to geographically 'zone' areas for collection, the task can be completed with an expenditure of physical energy equivalent to that of a pleasant, slightly testing, country walk.

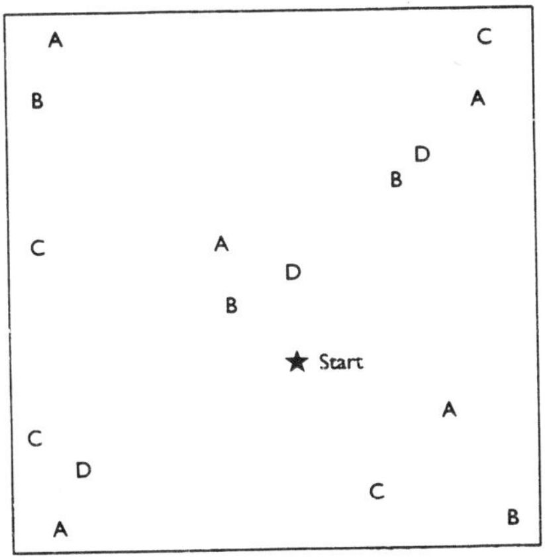

A typical layout of sites (not to scale).

Having identified the sites, write codewords of your own devising on the cards, and place them at the sites in question, making a note on the master map, or a separate list of which codewords have gone where. We always use codewords which start with the same letter as the classes. For example, for the A series we use the codewords *abacus*, *abracadabra*, *aeroplane*, *artist* and *Armenia*. The purpose of codewords is merely to identify which sites have been visited, to aid the clearing up process.

Unless you own the ground being used or have come to an agreement with the landowners, the cards should be placed less than 24 hours before the exercise and should bear a message to the effect that they are part of a training exercise and will be cleared away within 48 hours. The cards should be placed in places of legal access.

Mark the group maps with the various sites, and issue them together with the group brief, pens and notepads.

After the exercise, clear away any cards which have not been collected by the group.

GROUP NOTES

Trails and tribulations

Task Goodbill Harriers Ltd, a new leisure pursuits organization, is keen to develop orienteering holidays. The holidays are very firmly aimed at the family market, so each course must meet the needs of people across a whole range of orienteering skills. They are divided into four classes, ranging from 'Beginner' through 'Novice' and 'Intermediate', on up to 'Skilled' and – best of all – 'Expert'.

The company now wishes you to test 17 of the proposed sites in this area. They are willing to pay you for visiting checkpoints which are in the four classes and you should try to maximize income by collecting as many proofs of visit from the sites as possible. Each site is marked with its own codeword, written on a small card. Presentation of these cards to a member of course staff at the start/finish point constitutes the only acceptable proof of visit.

Differing rates of pay are offered for visiting different classes of site, as set out below:

	Checks	*Value per check*	*Completion bonus*	*Maximum value*
Class A	5	£0.50	£2.50	£5.00
Class B	4	£0.40	£2.40	£4.00
Class C	4	£0.30	£1.80	£3.00
Class D	4	£0.25	£1.50	£2.50

You must decide which class(es) to complete, and each group *must* tell the course staff *exactly* which sites they intend to visit before they set off.

There are penalties:

a) for each check missed on a course attempted – £0.50
b) for failure to return to base within 1 hour 45 minutes of the start time:
   i) up to 5 minutes late – £0.50 per offending person;
   ii) 5 to 10 minutes late – £1.20 per offending person;
   iii) over 10 minutes late – £0.80 per 5 minutes, or part thereof, per offending person.

Equipment

- ☐ 5 marked copies of the appropriate map. Please only annotate these in pencil or with the special pens provided. The start/finish point is also marked.
- ☐ pencils or special pens
- ☐ a small notebook for each team member.

Time 1 hour 45 minutes.

Safety

- Do not split into groups of less than three, and remain in sight and sound of each other at all times. This means that if one group member has a mishap, there is someone to stay with them and someone else to fetch help.
- Walking boots should be worn.
- Do not wear waterproofs on dry days (especially hot ones). Carry them in rucksacks if you wish.
- Give course staff a record of the planned routes and estimated time of return for each group member before you leave the start point.
- Take the drinks we have provided with you. *Do not under any circumstances* consume alcohol during the exercise – this dehydrates people.
- People suffering from heart, respiratory, or similar disorders should only take part in the planning phase of this task.

CHAPTER 8

WATER-BASED EXERCISES

29. A BRIDGED VERSION

Facilitator notes

A Bridged Version is a complex, phased exercise with a broad range of learning opportunities. Although it requires a lot of preparation time and equipment, the results more than justify it. The task involves the group building a pontoon bridge across a river or lake. You will need to identify a suitable location and adapt the exercise to your specific needs. The exercise breaks naturally into a number of phases, some distinct and others overlapping. It also provides a number of roles, including various leadership roles. The keys to success for the participants, as with so many large projects, are careful planning, clear roles and good communications. Possible applications include project management, leadership and delegation.

Numbers 12 to 20, with 3 to 5 facilitators/safety staff.

Time Effectively 24 hours.

Materials As appropriate to your chosen location, but as a guideline:

	Item		*Quantity*
☐	barrels plastic, large		12
☐	barrels plastic, small		20
☐	barrels steel		12
☐	base plates	*	12
☐	bicycles		2
☐	buoyancy aids		10
☐	calculators		2
☐	double couplers	*	310
☐	gloves hi-grip		20
☐	graph paper		1 pad
☐	karabiners		12
☐	model kit, consisting of balsa wood, pins and glue	#	1
☐	paddles		8
☐	pallets	*	10
☐	planks	*	various, totalling 330ft
☐	pulleys		4
☐	rope, 100ft lengths		6
☐	ropes, for lashing		30
☐	safety helmets		1 each
☐	scaffold poles, long	*	44 × 21ft
☐	scaffold poles, short	*	130 × 4ft
☐	scaffold spanners	*	8
☐	scientific calculator	#	1
☐	tape measures		2
☐	walkie talkies	#	2
☐	wheelchair		1

* These items can be hired from scaffold suppliers.

Some items are obviously optional, but add interest and realism. They may be deleted from the list, as other items can be added.

Set-up Identify a suitable site on a river or lake, with reasonable access and working space and not too much passing water traffic, although some can add an extra dimension to the exercise.

Obtain necessary access permission, remembering to include vehicular access for your transport and that of your scaffold supplier.

Order your heavy supplies for delivery by the scaffolding supplier, ideally to arrive on the morning of the exercise. Be sure to clarify unloading arrangements; some suppliers expect help. If so, this can be built into the exercise.

Procedure

1. Issue outline brief, supplement verbally and answer questions, as appropriate. Beware of answering too many detailed questions, and of giving information available through reconnaissance or in the detailed brief.
2. Escort people to the construction site, during the recce time, if requested.
3. Monitor planning and design, answering questions as appropriate.
4. Conduct training in lashing, scaffold construction and raft building.
5. Issue detailed brief to nominated leaders.
6. Monitor planning and design.
7. Monitor planning time and enforce cut off if appropriate.
8. During building monitor safety, observe, and take notes.
9. Facilitate a mid-exercise review.
10. Inspect raft bridge for safety, award certificates as appropriate.
11. Supervise safe dismantling.
12. Facilitate review.

Prior training Conduct training in lashing, scaffold construction, and raft building.

Safety

- A full safety briefing should be included in the verbal briefing and constant safety monitoring be conducted. It may even be appropriate to appoint a delegate as site safety supervisor with an appropriate brief.
- Normal safety rules for working with scaffolding apply (see p.47).

- Helmets and gloves should be worn at all times.
- Buoyancy aids should be worn when on or over water.
- Provide a safety boat, particularly when the raft is in action.
- Check raft and bridge for safety at all times and ban unsafe structures.

GROUP NOTES

A bridged version

Outline brief

Task To design and construct a bridge over the lake/river at ________

Specification The bridge must be able to support a bicycle or a wheelchair and allow passage to boats.

Timings Construction commences at 0900 tomorrow, and the bridge is to be complete by 1500.

Equipment A list of available equipment, its cost and location will be issued with the detailed brief.

Site access The construction site will be open from 2030–2100 tonight and from 0900–1600 tomorrow.

Skills Training in appropriate skills will be given in the main training room from 2000–2100 tonight.

Detailed brief A further, detailed briefing will be given at 2000 tonight, to be attended by a maximum of 3 members.

Detailed brief

Location The bridge is to be built across the lake/river at ___________
The exact crossing point will be indicated on the ground.

Task To design and construct a bridge across the lake. This task breaks down into the following phases:

1. Design the bridge and plan its construction.
2. Build a raft to transport building materials to the remote bank.
3. Build the bridge.
4. Bridge inspected for safety and specification.
5. Bridge opens for business.

Specification The bridge must:

- be safely negotiable by a cyclist without dismounting;
- be safely negotiable by a person pushed in a wheelchair;
- allow passage by boats with masts, and up to 5 feet abeam.

Timings

0700	Breakfast.
0800	Exercise starts.
0900	Site opens.
1100–1200	Mid-exercise review.
1500	Completion deadline.
1600	Bridge dismantled, site closes.

Equipment See Annex A.

Completion When completed to your satisfaction the bridge will be inspected and, if satisfactory, awarded a safety certificate. It will then be inspected for compliance to specification. You will remain responsible for the bridge until the customer has accepted it as complete as specified. You must inform the training staff when you are ready for inspection and be prepared to assist in trials.

Finances The contract price for the bridge is £1000. A bonus will be paid for early completion at a rate of £100 per 15 minutes. Equipment costs are at Annex A. You have an unlimited overdraft facility for the duration of the exercise.

Domestics Packed lunches will be provided by the hotel. An office with tea making facilities is available on site.

Safety Everyone should be aware of the need for safe working procedures when handling equipment or working near water and act responsibly. The following rules also apply and violation may be penalized.

- Training staff retain final authority on safety and their directions must be followed at all times.
- Helmets to be worn at all times in the construction areas.
- Buoyancy aids must be worn while on the water, on a raft, or on the bridge, until it has a safety certificate.
- Damage to the site must be minimal and no vegetation damaged.
- Adequate provision for, and consideration to, members of the public must be given. This may involve liaison with other groups.

If in doubt ask the training staff.

The customer The training staff will at times adopt the role of customer or safety inspector. Their intention is neither to confuse nor hinder, but to make the most of the exercise for you. Please assist them in this awkward dual role.

Annex A: Equipment list

	Item	*Quantity*	*Price*	*Located*
☐	Barrels plastic, large	12	50p each	site
☐	Barrels plastic, small	20	25p each	site
☐	barrels steel	12	£1.00 each	site
☐	base plates	12	10p each	site
☐	buoyancy aids	10	50p each	site
☐	bicycle	2	£5.00	base
☐	calculator	2	50p each	base
☐	calculator, scientific	1	£1.00	base
☐	double couplers	310	10p each	site
☐	gloves hi-grip	20	20p/pair	base
☐	graph paper		5p/sheet	base
☐	helmets, safety		free	base
☐	karabiners	12	25p each	base
☐	model kit	1	£3.00	base
☐	paddles	8	50p	site
☐	pallets	10	50p each	site
☐	planks	330ft	10p/ft	site
☐	pulleys	4	25p each	base
☐	rope		10p/metre	base
☐	scaffold poles, long	44 × 21ft	5p/ft	site
☐	scaffold poles, short	130 × 4ft	5p/ft	site
☐	scaffold spanners	8	£2.00 each	base
☐	tape measures	2	50p each	base
☐	walkie talkies	2	£2.50 each	base
☐	wheelchair	1	£10.00	base

If anything you need is not on the list, please ask.

30. Beecher's Brook

Facilitator notes

Crossing a river by means of a 'Beechers' Buoy' on a taut rope can be more physical than many of the exercises described here. It can also, if set up well, be achieved by all people regardless of physical fitness – although it is inadvisable to force anybody to attempt it, and we always write in an escape clause for people with genuine fears or physical weaknesses. Although not actually dangerous, it can be very daunting, and therefore provides a huge sense of achievement which can be very useful for team-building.

You will need to identify a suitable stretch of river (or stream or lake) and amend the brief as necessary. The location needs at least one strong tree on either bank from which to suspend the rope. The trees should be far enough back from the bank to allow people to clip onto the rope safely and easily. Be sure to obtain access permission from both landowners.

The river or other waterway need not be deep or fast-flowing, although this increases the challenge. The constraints and boundary definition are the real keys to complexity. Careful definition of the boundaries can eliminate dangerous areas, limit or increase the choice of trees to be used, and even legislate for dry river beds!

There are also many simple alternatives to embellish the brief, such as being required to take items across.

Numbers 6 to 18.

Time 1–2 hours.

Materials

- ☐ 3 × 30m (100ft) ropes
- ☐ light throwing line
- ☐ 6 × karabiners
- ☐ 4 × harnesses (various sizes)
- ☐ 4 × canoe helmets (various sizes)
- ☐ 4 × buoyancy aids (various sizes)
- ☐ 2 × slings
- ☐ gloves

Procedure

1. Brief team.
2. Take team to crossing site.
3. Clarify boundaries.
4. Monitor safety.

Prior training Knots, rope usage, rope tightening, fitting of harnesses.

Variations

- 2 teams operating from opposite banks.
- Separate planning and execution phases.
- Cargo to transport.

Safety

- This exercise should be supervised by appropriately skilled and experienced staff.
- Ensure knots and equipment are properly fitted and secured.
- Ensure appropriate equipment worn.
- Watch for over-enthusiasm in pulling ropes, thus trapping fingers or causing burns.

GROUP NOTES

Beecher's brook

Task For the entire team (subject to constraints) to cross the river within the boundaries indicated.

Time 90 minutes.

Equipment

- ☐ 3 × 30m (100ft) ropes
- ☐ throwing line
- ☐ 6 × karabiners
- ☐ 2 × slings
- ☐ harnesses
- ☐ helmets
- ☐ buoyancy aids
- ☐ gloves.

Constraints

- No one and no equipment other than the throwing line may get wet.
- All knots are to be checked by safety staff.
- A helmet, buoyancy aid and harness must be worn while crossing.
- Up to 2 team members may remain on the original bank to aid dismantling.

31. Cash float

Facilitator notes

Cash Float is a task in which the groups build rafts and race them against each other. Apart from the obvious teamwork, a further element of management is introduced by the fact that equipment has to be bought. There is a real chance that a thrifty team will come last in the race and still make more money than the winners.

Numbers Around 12 works best, but the task can be achieved (with varying results) by group numbers as low as 6 or as high as 20. We have specified equipment for 12. This should remain the same for smaller groups and increase by around 50% of everything for the larger group.

Time Allow 1 hour 45 minutes.

Materials (enough for two groups):

- ☐ 8 × empty 115-litre (25-gall.) containers (watertight)
- ☐ 6 × empty 200-litre (45-gall.) containers (watertight)
- ☐ 14 × 2.5m (8ft) wooden poles
- ☐ 10 × canoe paddles
- ☐ around 80 × 3m (10ft) 5mm polypropylene ropes
- ☐ buoyancy aids/lifejackets for all
- ☐ canoeing helmets for all
- ☐ industrial safety gloves for all
- ☐ notebooks and pens/pencils for all
- ☐ a marker buoy
- ☐ safety boat (for staff use)

Procedure Take the group to the appropriate lake/river bank, where the material should previously have been laid out. Brief the leader/group and answer any amplifying questions, but push back to the group any questions seeking methods for actually doing the task. Announce to the group that you are starting the clock, and it's over to them. Stop and review after the given time or when the group has completed the task, whichever is the sooner.

Prior training Rafts are always built more efficiently if some (say half) of the group have received training in making square and diagonal lashings. A less adequate substitute is to provide the group with a book or other handout on how to do this.

Safety

- Any raft built should be checked by safety staff before launching, to assess its waterworthiness. Safety staff should have the power to veto the launch of any vessel built, on grounds of safety. In doing so, they should act like the Health and Safety Inspectorate, offering advice as well as criticism.
- A safety boat should be on the water at all times when rafts are being launched or sailed. For preference, this should be powered by an engine but, given the low speed of rafts, stable rowing boats are an acceptable substitute on still water.
- Buoyancy aids (for strong swimmers) and full lifejackets (for weak swimmers) are a must. Ensure that waistbelts are secured on these, as otherwise there is a risk of the wearer and the aid becoming separated. Most outdoor trainers possess these items, which should be checked for continued buoyancy on a regular basis, as they are subject to deterioration with continued use.
- Have a full safety sack (see p.41) available, together with some large towels.
- Instruct the group to bring a change of dry clothes with them. They must wear plimsolls or trainers on their feet, as these are light. Boots, especially wellingtons, can fill with water and cause people to be pulled under.
- Bring a large flask of tea or coffee.
- Ensure that you know the provenance of any 25- or 45-gallon drums used. These are best when bought new or from a responsible secondhand dealer who will have 'reamed' the inside very fully.
- Someone with a throwing line on the bank is a very useful backup to the safety boat. Such lines are available from outdoor shops.

GROUP NOTES

Cash float

Cash Float is a task with a clear purpose: to make as much money as is safely possible by building and racing a raft – which must carry a minimum of 4 people at all times – from the start point (indicated by staff), around the marker buoy, and back to the start. The race starts now, and there are cash prizes for first (£30.00) and second (£25.00) place. Materials are available at the costs set out below:

Materials and costs

This is the total material available to both groups:

- ☐ 8 × empty 115-litre (25-gall.) containers (watertight) @ £1.50 each
- ☐ 6 × empty 200-litre (45-gall.) containers (watertight) @ £2.25 each
- ☐ 14 × 2.5m (8ft) wooden poles @ 50p each
- ☐ 10 × canoe paddles @ £1.00 each
- ☐ around 80 × 3m (10ft) 5mm polypropylene ropes @ £3.00 per batch of 10 (We will not sell smaller batches, and no group can buy more than 4 batches.)
- ☐ buoyancy aids/lifejackets for all (free)
- ☐ canoeing helmets for all (free)
- ☐ industrial safety gloves for all (free)
- ☐ notebooks and pens/pencils for all (free)

Safety See notes provided.

32. Deliverance

Facilitator notes

The simplicity of this idea belies its potential for fun and learning. Organized properly, it can cover many aspects of communication, teamwork and leadership. The exercise is a competitive canoe relay, with constraints to maximize learning and involvement.

Although the basic exercise would work with kayaks, there is more learning potential, more teamwork, less training and less fear if you use open Canadian canoes. These open boats are more stable and can take more people, 2 or 3 very comfortably.

Numbers 8 to 18 in teams of 4 to 6.

Time 60–90 minutes.

Materials

To set up

- ☐ buoys or floats (2 per team). An ice-cream tub secured with string and rock will suffice.
- ☐ tennis-balls or similar small objects (6 per float)
- ☐ prizes, if appropriate
- ☐ safety boat
- ☐ whistle

For group use

- ☐ buoyancy aids
- ☐ canoe helmets

- ☐ paddles
- ☐ canoes
- ☐ towels and dry clothes.

Set-up Place 2 floats per team on the water, with 6 tennis balls in each, at some distance from the bank and from each other.

Procedure

1. Brief teams.
2. Allow planning time.
3. Start race.
4. Monitor safety and rules.
5. Decide winner and award prizes.

Prior training Water safety (see pages 41–43) and handling a canoe.

Safety All the usual water safety rules apply; a safety boat should be on the water at all times.

GROUP NOTES

Deliverance

Task To collect tennis balls from the floats on the lake.

Objective To collect more tennis balls than the other team(s).

Time 15 minutes' planning time and 30 minutes' execution time.

Constraints

- Only one ball from each float may be carried in the canoe at a time.
- Each team member must make at least one trip.
- No more than 3 people at a time may go in each canoe.
- Everyone in the canoe must wear a buoyancy aid and helmet.
- No one is to intentionally enter the water.
- If the exercise controller blows the whistle everyone must stop and listen for instructions. The exercise is suspended until restarted.

Safety Refer to separate safety notes.

33. ENDEAVOURANCE

Facilitator notes

This exercise is a canoe expedition along a river or canal and needs considerable careful preparation for success and safety. Inadequate preparation may lead to unnecessary danger, or to unpleasant encounters with angry landowners, which will at least detract from learning and damage your credibility. Choose a section of river with no dangerous stretches and a number of possible landing points with road or footpath access. Physically check all access points for practicality and legality, seeking permission where necessary, checking from the river and the road.

Numbers 12 or more.

Time 12 hours.

Materials

- ☐ 4 × canoes
- ☐ 8 × paddles
- ☐ 12 × buoyancy aids
- ☐ 12 × canoe helmets
- ☐ maps
- ☐ compasses
- ☐ waterproof map-covers
- ☐ sounding lines
- ☐ canoe trailer
- ☐ minibus with towing hook
- ☐ packed lunches
- ☐ tea-making facilities

Procedure Having reconnoitred the river, roads and all access points, amend the brief as necessary. There should, where feasible, be more possible staging points than required in the brief. Brief the delegates, answer questions and provide advice during the planning phase. Be ready to take everyone to the launch point at the appointed time. Thereafter the delegates should direct operations, although the safety staff on the water and the minibus driver retain power of veto on all safety issues.

Prior training Some prior instruction by properly qualified trainers (BCU or its overseas equivalent) is essential.

Safety All canoe and water safety rules (see pages 41–43) apply, and should be briefed to the teams.

GROUP NOTES

Endeavourance

Task You are to plan and execute a canoe trip along the river ________, starting at ________________ and finishing at ________________.

The route is to have at least ____ staging points, where the canoes will be met by a support party travelling by road. Each stage is to be at least 1 kilometre long, and not more than 3 kilometres. The canoes must remain together at all times, and will be accompanied by safety staff in their own craft. All canoe safety rules must be observed.

You are to take soundings every 500m and under every bridge on the route and keep a record of these soundings. You will also write a report on the accessibility of staging points, with particular reference to vehicular access and suitability for launching and recovering canoes.

The support party will travel by minibus. The driver is provided, but you are expected to navigate. You will provide hot drinks at a minimum of two of the staging points. You must not trespass or in any way break the law.

Time You have 1 hour to plan and should be ready to leave for the launch point by ________.

Equipment available

- ☐ 4 × canoes
- ☐ 8 × paddles
- ☐ 12 × buoyancy aids
- ☐ 12 × canoe helmets
- ☐ maps
- ☐ compasses

- [ ] waterproof map-covers
- [ ] sounding lines
- [ ] canoe trailer
- [ ] minibus and driver
- [ ] packed lunches
- [ ] tea-making facilities.

Safety

- Helmets and buoyancy aids (for strong swimmers) or full lifejackets (for weak swimmers) are a must. Ensure that waistbelts are secured on these, as otherwise there is a risk of the wearer and the aid becoming separated.
- A full safety sack is available, together with some large towels.
- Bring a change of dry clothes with you. You should also wear plimsolls or trainers on your feet, as these are light.
- A large flask of tea or coffee is available, for emergency use only.

34. Necessary measures

Facilitator notes

Necessary Measures is a task in which the group conducts a survey of a lake or river bed, with the objective of making a presentation to course staff/invited guests on their findings.

Numbers Around 12 works best, but the task can be achieved (with varying results) by group numbers as low as 6 or as high as 20. We have specified equipment for 12. This should remain the same for smaller groups and increase by around 50% of everything for the larger group.

Time Allow between 3 and 4 hours, depending on group size (4 hours for 6–9 members, 3 hours 30 minutes for 10–15 members, 3 hours for 16 or more). The time includes the survey and the presentation.

Materials

For the survey

- ☐ 8 × empty 115-litre (25-gall.) containers (watertight) *or*
- ☐ 6 × empty 200-litre (45-gall.) containers (watertight)
- ☐ 10 × 2.5m (8ft) wooden poles
- ☐ 8 × canoe paddles (various sizes)
- ☐ 4 × 30m (100ft) 8mm ropes
- ☐ 50 × 3m (10ft) 5mm polypropylene ropes
- ☐ 1 × surveyors' tape-measure
- ☐ buoyancy aids/lifejackets for all

- ☐ canoeing helmets for all
- ☐ industrial safety gloves for all
- ☐ 4 × notebooks and pens/pencils
- ☐ a 1:50,000 scale map showing the lake/river
- ☐ safety boat for staff use.

For the presentation

- ☐ flipchart, pens and paper
- ☐ overhead projector complete with foils and pens (optional).

Procedure Take the group to the appropriate lake/river bank where the material should previously have been laid out. Hand out the group brief and allow 10 minutes for reading it and understanding the task. Answer any amplifying questions, but push back to the group any questions seeking methods for actually doing the task. After 10 minutes announce to the group that you are starting the clock, and it's over to them. Stop and review after the given time or when the group has completed the task, whichever is the sooner.

Prior training Rafts are always built more efficiently if some (say half) the group have received training in making square and diagonal lashings. A less adequate substitute is to provide the group with a book or other handout on how to do this.

Safety

- Any raft built should be checked by safety staff before launching, to assess its waterworthiness. Safety staff should have the power to veto the launch of any vessel built, on grounds of safety. In doing so, they should act like the Health and Safety Inspectorate, offering advice as well as criticism.
- A safety boat should be on the water at all times when rafts are being launched or sailed. For preference, this should be powered by an engine but, given the low speed of rafts, stable rowing boats are an acceptable substitute on still waters.
- Buoyancy aids (for strong swimmers) and full lifejackets (for weak swimmers) are a must. Ensure that waistbelts are secured on these, as otherwise there is a risk of the wearer and the aid becoming separated. Most outdoor trainers possess these items,

which should be checked for continued buoyancy on a regular basis, as they are subject to deterioration with continued use.

- Have a full safety sack (see p.41) available, together with some large towels.
- Instruct the group to bring a change of dry clothes with them. They must wear plimsolls or trainers on their feet, as these are light. Boots, especially wellingtons, can fill with water and cause people to be pulled under.
- Bring a large flask of tea or coffee.
- Someone with a throwing line on the bank is a very useful backup to the safety boat. Such lines are available from outdoor shops.

GROUP NOTES

Necessary measures

Necessary Measures is a task with a clear purpose: to make a presentation on the geography/topology of the surface and floor of the lake within ______ minutes. To amplify, Key Result Areas are:

- 5 or more profiles of the lake floor, from side to side;
- a map to 1:2500 scale of the surface of the lake, with the survey lines shown on it;
- a formal presentation of your findings.

Your performance in the task will be assessed on:

- quality (accuracy and detail) and quantity of the profiles of the lake. Survey points should be at most 3m (10ft) apart on each survey line, and lines should be within 10m (33ft) of each other.
- quality (accuracy and detail) of the map;
- quality (clarity and interest) of the presentation.

Materials

- ☐ 8 × empty 115-litre (25-gall.) containers (watertight) *or*
- ☐ 6 × empty 200-litre (45-gall.) containers (watertight)
- ☐ 10 × 2.5m (8ft) wooden poles
- ☐ 8 × canoe paddles (various sizes)
- ☐ 4 × 30m (100ft) 8mm ropes
- ☐ 50 × 3m (10ft) 5mm polypropylene ropes
- ☐ 1 × surveyors' tape-measure
- ☐ buoyancy aids, gloves, and helmets as required (available for all)

- ☐ 4 × notebooks and pens/pencils
- ☐ a 1:50,000 scale map of the area
- ☐ flipchart, paper and pens.

Other presentation material (overhead projector, viewfoils and pens) may also be available at base. Check with staff.

Safety See safety notes provided.

35. Off the hook

Facilitator notes

Retrieving a buoy from a lake or pond with limited equipment, and with neither people nor equipment touching the water, requires a minimum of set-up for a wealth of learning. This is an exercise with a simple solution, requiring good coordination of the team for success. Its simplicity is one of its strengths, as it generates useful review material that is easily related back to work for most delegates. The problems and frustrations of completing a simple task or solving a minor problem are readily recognizable.

Numbers 4 to 8.

Time 30–45 minutes.

Materials

To set up the task

- ☐ 1 buoy or other buoyant container with handle or 'eye'.

For group use

- ☐ 2 × 2m (6ft) poles
- ☐ 1 × 3m (10ft) pole
- ☐ ropes and string for lashing
- ☐ tent peg or similar to act as a hook.

Set-up Position the buoy approx. 4m (12ft) from the bank, anchored to limit drift and movement. Lay the equipment on the bank.

Procedure Take group to bank and brief.

Safety Beware of participants being careless at the water's edge. If appropriate to the location, brief the group on pertinent rules and/or issue Group Notes on safety in water-based activities.

GROUP NOTES

Off the hook

Task To retrieve the buoy from the lake. Neither people nor equipment may touch the water, and you may use only the equipment provided.

Time 30 minutes.

Resources

- ☐ 3 poles
- ☐ string
- ☐ rope
- ☐ tent pegs.

36. Plato

Facilitator notes

PLATO (Pipe Line Above The Ocean) is a task in which a group works to divert a stream, or part of it, across a pond or lake by means of a pipeline which they have to design and build. The pipeline should end at a point where the water contained in it will flow harmlessly away. The best location of all for the outflow is the usual exit-point for the lake's water.

Numbers 10 to 25 in the basic form of the exercise; more in embellished variations. (Up to 70 have been involved at once.)

Time Variable, depending on the size of the stream, lake and group numbers. At least 6 hours, but up to 3 days with variations.

Safety See safety in water-based activities, pages 41–43.

Set-up Once a suitable large pond or lake has been identified and access agreed, there is surprisingly little set-up effort for the basic exercise. The major effort is in acquiring the necessary equipment and transporting it to a site close to the operational area.

Equipment

- ☐ sufficient 15cm (6in.) rigid plastic pipes to reach from a suitable point in the stream to the far side of the lake
- ☐ enough 10cm (4in.) carpet tape to seal the connections between the pipes

- ☐ 1.70m (6ft) wooden stakes (6 × the number of pipes)
- ☐ 200-litre (45-gall.) drums (2 × the number of pipes)
- ☐ rowing boats: one 4-seater per 10 group members. (Providing sufficient qualified staff are available and group members have received effective training, Canadian canoes or kayaks are an effective substitute.)
- ☐ raft-building materials for one 4-person raft per 10 delegates. (See exercise *Cash Float* for detailed list.)
- ☐ canoeing helmets, buoyancy aids/life jackets and gloves for all
- ☐ a very large quantity of twine
- ☐ scissors and knives
- ☐ a roll of strong, layflat polyethylene tubing. (The best is of about the same thickness as fertilizer bags.)
- ☐ 15 × 2m (6ft) wooden planks.

Set-up Once a suitable large pond or lake has been identified and access agreed, there is surprisingly little set-up effort for the basic exercise. The major effort is in acquiring the necessary equipment and transporting it to a site close to the operational area.

Procedure As the exercise can be quite complex, we recommend a verbal briefing to either the full group or the leader. This should be supported by a written brief which can also form your speaking notes. Essentially, however, once the group has received the brief it's up to them to do the task.

We recommend for all longer exercises that the group reviews at around 3-hourly intervals (2-hourly in the case of a 6-hour exercise). The final review should take place as soon as possible after the task, but allow time for clearing away and cleaning up.

As the exercise may well cut across mealtimes, groups will need to be informed about the appropriate arrangements and times.

Prior training No prior training is required, although rafts are always better if some training in knots, lashings and basic stability has taken place. If Canadian canoes or kayaks are to be used, prior instruction by properly BCU (or its overseas equivalent) qualified trainers is a 'must'.

Variations There are many variations to this exercise. The principal ones are listed below:

- By way of training in 'new wave' production management, set the exercise up so that groups are forced to work in a traditional manner, with sales, design and manufacturing departments all working to tight briefs, communicating reasonably freely at 'board' level but rarely – if at all – at production worker level. Once the group becomes frustrated with this method of organization, set them free to organize how they wish. This should lead them to adopt the commonsense procedures that underlie the new wave approach – clustering around the problem, kanban, and so on – which in turn leads them to accept the need to work that way back in the business.

  With effective facilitation this can be a most powerful tool for turning resistors of change into agents of change.
- The exercise can be turned into a fully-fledged business game. Constructing the pipeline is a central task which must be achieved, but the hardware for it must be purchased with the income earned by performing a compendium of smaller tasks.

  This version is much more complex than the basic one, with loans being offered, interest rates changed, proper accounts kept, payment for stages, and so on. In many ways building the pipeline is only one part – albeit a vital one – of the task. This version of the exercise has kept groups of 70 busy for up to 3 days.
- Scenarios ranging from the most simple to the most complex can be devised to meet particular training needs.

GROUP NOTES

Plato

Task You are to divert a stream from its entry point at G.R. _________ across the large pond/lake into which it would normally flow, by means of a pipeline which you have to design and build. The pipeline should leave the lake at G.R. ____________. It may not be built on land around the edge of the pond/lake, it *must* cross the waters of the lake.

Equipment

- ☐ sufficient 15cm (6in.) rigid plastic pipes to reach from a suitable point in the stream to the far side of the lake
- ☐ enough 10cm (4in.) carpet tape to seal the connections between the pipes
- ☐ 1.70m (6ft) wooden stakes (6 × the number of pipes)
- ☐ 200-litre (45-gall.) drums (2 × the number of pipes)
- ☐ rowing boats/Canadian canoes/kayaks
- ☐ raft-building materials
- ☐ canoeing helmets, buoyancy aids/life jackets and gloves for all
- ☐ a very large quantity of twine
- ☐ scissors and knives
- ☐ a roll of strong, layflat polyethylene tubing
- ☐ 15 × 2m (6ft) wooden planks.

Maximum time allowed _______________

CHAPTER 9

CLIFF-FACE EXERCISES

37. HAUL OF FAME

Facilitator notes

Haul of Fame is a task in which two groups standing within a few yards of each other compete or co-operate to perform 'units' of abseils and mountain rescue hauls, for which they earn money for charity.

Numbers 10 to 16.

Time 2 hours 30 minutes.

Equipment for this exercise should be provided by safety staff, and should include sufficient ropes to allow 2 groups simultaneously to abseil or haul, with the appropriate safety ropes, rigging ropes, harnesses, belts, helmets, gloves, etc. In addition, you should provide a notebook and pen/pencil for each delegate.

Procedure Either issue the brief for the task to the groups when you reach the cliff-face or, if travelling to the site in separate vehicles, issue the briefs once the vehicles are under way. This gives each group the opportunity to consider options away from the influence of the other. Once they arrive at the site, issue personal safety gear and insist that all – even those with no desire to go up or down the cliff-face – wear them all the time whilst at the site. Show them their work area, verbally underline the safety tutors' role, answer any questions they may have, and it's over to them.

Prior training can vary from none at all (but with group access to written notes on relevant climbing technology) right through to every delegate having abseiled under the control of a safety tutor.

We usually opt for a middle course where some have received hands-on training in hauling, some in abseiling, and others in safety-rope procedures. Typically, this will have been in a less-than-real situation, perhaps a hotel garden or group room. The advantage of this approach is that the groups as a whole have all the necessary knowledge, but no one individual is an expert. This, combined with the reality of the situation, encourages a healthy sharing of knowledge.

Variations

- With sufficient trainers, equipment and a big enough cliff, the exercise can run with 3 or more groups, adding a very powerful group dynamic to the whole thing.
- With a smaller group a one-team variation is possible.

Safety See pages 44–46 and issue Group Notes on safety in cliff-face exercises.

Set-up Site-finding is the most difficult part. Be sure you do this in partnership with a safety tutor who knows the area. The climbing guidebooks which are published for most likely districts are invaluable, both for identifying sites and clarifying access requirements. Most areas in which outdoor pursuits centres operate have crags to which centres and others have access.

Once a site has been identified and access agreed, setting up is usually a simple matter of sending one safety tutor ahead to rig the belays and transport the climbing equipment to the group pitches.

GROUP NOTES

Haul of fame

Task To produce as large a profit as possible by performing 'units' of abseils and hauls. You will be paid £0.60 for each completed 'unit' of one abseil *and* one haul, up to a maximum of 8 units. A bonus of £1.20 is payable if each group member completes either one abseil or one haul, or handles the safety rope for more than 15 minutes.

You may purchase tuition on ropework from safety staff at the rate of one additional unit per five minutes or part thereof that tutors spend answering questions. Tutors will not volunteer information, except for safety reasons.

At the end of the time allowed, your score will be multiplied by that of the other team, and the final figure paid to a charity of your choice. Should you sustain a loss, *you* will have to pay the charity of *our* choice. An example is set out below:

Group A		**Group B**	
completes 5 units	£3.00	completes 8 units	£4.80
less 2 safety fines	(£1.20)	*less* 1 safety fine	£0.60
	£1.80		£4.20
less tuition (10 mins)	£1.20	*less* tuition (10 mins)	£1.20
Total, Group A:	£0.60	*plus* completion bonus	£1.20
		Total, Group B	£4.20

The two groups' totals multiplied together come to £2.52.

Equipment is set out at your group's operating site. In addition, every group member should wear a safety helmet and climbing belt.

Maximum time allowed 2 hours 30 minutes.

Safety Detailed safety notes are attached, and should be read and understood by all group members.

38. Rock compilation

Facilitator notes

Rock Compilation is a business game in which the group gains income by two means:

1. Making a presentation of between 15 and 20 minutes on some aspect of the history of the area which involves rock. It might be related to climbing, mining, rock extraction, geology or whatever.
2. Making ascents (by climbing) and descents (by abseiling) of crags in the area.

Numbers 10 to 18.

Time 7 hours, including presentation time.

Equipment Technical equipment for this exercise should be provided by safety staff, and should be sufficient to allow 2 groups simultaneously to abseil or climb, with the appropriate safety ropes, rigging ropes, harnesses, belts, helmet, gloves etc.

In addition, you should provide:

- ☐ a notebook and pen/pencil for each delegate
- ☐ 3 × 1:50,000 scale maps of the area
- ☐ a local climbing guide with suitable crags marked and graded into 3 levels of difficulty (Easy, Medium and Hard)
- ☐ a list of local museums, show-mines and other sites of relevance
- ☐ a budget (£20.00) to spend on leaflets and books
- ☐ any relevant books you may possess
- ☐ appropriate presentation equipment
- ☐ appropriate transport and drivers for the group
- ☐ a packed lunch and tea/coffee for all.

Procedure To avoid distractions, brief the leader or group in a training room, preferably a few miles from any usable crags. Once the brief has been issued, it's over to them. The exercise concludes with a presentation to course staff on the rock-related historical item. After this, allow time for cleaning up before reviewing.

Prior training Can vary from none at all (but with group access to written notes on the relevant climbing technology) right through to every delegate having climbed and abseiled under the control of a safety tutor.

Variations The exercise has great flexibility and can be tailored to a variety of needs. Typical variants are:

- a two- or multi-group option, in which presentations are made to other groups as well as course staff;
- a video presentation instead of the usual flipchart-and-overhead projector type;
- a change of focus so that the presentation is on the learning benefits of outdoor exercises rather than on historical matters.

Safety Issue notes on safety in cliff-face exercises. (see pages 44–46.)

Set-up Site-finding is the most difficult and time-consuming part. Be sure you do this in partnership with a safety tutor who knows the area. The climbing guidebooks which are published for most likely districts are invaluable, both for identifying sites and clarifying access requirements. Most areas in which outdoor pursuits centres operate have crags to which centres and others have access.

Most areas with sufficient crags also boast a fair supply of show-caves and mines, and museums are multiplying so quickly that almost every locality in the land possesses one.

Once sites have been identified and access agreed, setting up is a matter of ensuring that any group going out is accompanied by a safety tutor (who can also drive for them) and has the correct equipment.

GROUP NOTES

Rock compilation

Task A business game in which you gain income by two means:

1. Making a presentation on some aspect of the history of the area which involves rock. It might be related to climbing, mining, rock extraction, geology or whatever. The detailed subject-matter is up to you.
2. Making ascents (by climbing) and descents (by abseiling) of crags in the area.

Equipment provided for your team is as follows:

- ☐ appropriate technical equipment for two groups simultaneously to abseil or climb, with the appropriate safety ropes, rigging ropes, harnesses, belts, helmet, gloves, etc.
- ☐ a notebook and pen/pencil for each delegate
- ☐ 3 × 1:50,000 scale maps of the area
- ☐ a local climbing guide with the available crags marked
- ☐ a list of local museums, show-mines and other sites of relevance
- ☐ a budget (£20.00) to spend on leaflets and books
- ☐ relevant books
- ☐ appropriate presentation equipment
- ☐ appropriate transport and drivers for the group
- ☐ a packed lunch and tea/coffee for all.

Maximum time allowed 7 hours, including presentation time.

Income is generated in two ways:

1. *By abseiling and climbing.* There are three levels of income for climbing, based on the difficulty of the climb:

   - Easy climbs: 40 points per person
   - Medium climbs: 70 points per person
   - Hard climbs: 100 points per person

   Likewise, there are two levels of income for abseiling:

   - short abseils: 35 points per person
   - long abseils: 80 points per person

2. *For the presentation:* up to 1200 points to be awarded by staff, based upon:

   - quality of presentation (including effective use of visual aids);
   - factual content and accuracy;
   - duration (aim for between 15 and 20 minutes).

Expenditure

- Mileage travelled in the vehicles provided is charged at 15 points per mile.
- There is a 'green fee' of 80 points per crag attempted. The fee covers abseiling and climbing if these are available at the same site.
- Potential major infringements of safety rules will be subject to the intervention of safety staff before you are at risk. Minor infringements will be fined at a rate of 60 points per infringement.

Safety Detailed notes are attached. You should be sure that you read and understand these.

39. Up Pompeii

Facilitator notes

Climbing is an individual activity, but can be used for team development work if the exercise is carefully designed and properly reviewed. This is one such. Having identified a suitable crag, the exercise is effectively run by the delegates.

Numbers 6 to 18.

Time 1–2 hours.

Equipment

- ☐ climbing equipment, including all ropes and safety equipment
- ☐ climbing helmets
- ☐ harnesses
- ☐ climbing guide.

Procedure The group may be briefed before arrival to allow planning, or on the site. Safety staff then rig climbs as required.

Prior training Use of equipment, fitting of helmets and harnesses.

Safety See pages 44–46, and issue Group Notes on safety in cliff-face exercises. All crag safety procedures must be rigorously enforced and correct staff ratios observed.

GROUP NOTES

Up Pompeii

The task is to climb up or abseil down climbs at ______________ Crag. There is a variable reward, dependent on difficulty and severity of climbs, with a 50% bonus for each 'first ascent'.

Earnings

- Moderate 250 points
- Difficult 300
- Very Difficult 350
- Severe 450
- Hard Severe 500
- Hard Very Severe 600
- Extremely Severe 500 plus E × 100 points.
  (Where E is the technical difficulty grade of the climb, Extremely Severe climbs being further divided into grades E1 to E8. Thus an E3 climb is worth 800 points.)
- Abseil on any route 500

Constraints In addition to the attached safety notes, further restrictions may be applied by safety staff; please consult them if in doubt. For instance, the crag may be used by other climbers and normal rules of climbing etiquette must be observed; some routes may not be suitable for abseiling and some climbs may be declared unfit for use.

CHAPTER 10

UNDERGROUND EXERCISES

40. THE DANGEROUS DINERS CLUB

Facilitator notes

Virtually any activity or exercise can be made more challenging, exciting and demanding by being performed in a cave. The cave must be well mapped, known to your safety staff and suitable in terms of safety and ecology for the task envisaged. As with all such activities it is important to provide a role for those who prefer not to go underground, such as the cooking role detailed in the group notes. This task, to serve a meal underground, is great fun and very memorable. The cave used must have a suitable chamber or area inside to serve the meal and a suitable area outside for cooking. A tent or other shelter may be necessary in inclement weather. There is also an opportunity for delegates to show some initiative and creativity by providing entertainment.

Numbers 8 to 12.

Time 1–2 hours.

Materials

- ☐ caving helmets
- ☐ caving lamps
- ☐ boilersuits
- ☐ wellington boots
- ☐ first aid kit
- ☐ tent (optional)
- ☐ candles
- ☐ field telephone (optional); available from Army Surplus stores
- ☐ table and chairs (collapsible)
- ☐ crockery and cutlery
- ☐ meal-making facilities, cooker, fuel, etc.
- ☐ food
- ☐ camera (optional).

Variations

- Cook the meal underground.
- Make a presentation.
- Deliver an object to a specific location.
- Retrieve an object from a specific location.

Safety Normal cave safety rules apply, including staff ratios (see pp.50–53). Issue Group Notes on safety in underground exercises. Take particular care when other activities are occupying minds.

GROUP NOTES

The Dangerous Diners Club

Task To serve a three-course dinner to 4 invited guests in the ________ chamber of ______________ cave at ______________ tonight.

Constraints

- All cooking is to be done above ground.
- All equipment and rubbish must be removed from the cave and its vicinity on completion.
- Any enhancements to the occasion will be rewarded.

Equipment

- ☐ helmets
- ☐ caving lamps
- ☐ boilersuits
- ☐ wellington boots
- ☐ first aid kit
- ☐ candles
- ☐ field telephone
- ☐ table and chairs
- ☐ crockery and cutlery
- ☐ cooker and fuel
- ☐ food
- ☐ camera.

Safety You must observe at least in pairs at all times. Safety rules (attached) must be strictly observed.

41. District and circle

Facilitator notes

Exploring a cave can be very challenging and exciting for groups. You must choose a cave or system that is well mapped and known to your safety staff. The cave should be large enough to occupy the entire team for the allotted time. It may be necessary to supplement the restrictions in the brief to suit local conditions, such as prohibiting anyone from climbing pitches over 1m high. As with all such activities, it is important to provide a role for those who prefer not to go underground, such as the recording role detailed in the group notes.

Numbers 4 to 18.

Time 1–2 hours.

Equipment

- ☐ helmets
- ☐ caving lamps
- ☐ boilersuits
- ☐ wellington boots
- ☐ first aid kit
- ☐ clip-boards
- ☐ pencils and paper
- ☐ tea-making facilities (not flasks)

Safety Normal cave safety rules apply, including staff ratios (see pages 50–53). Issue Group Notes on safety in underground exercises.

GROUP NOTES

District and Circle

Task To explore as much of the cave system at __________ as possible in the time allowed. Make particular note of the following:

- other entrances/exits;
- pitches (climbs);
- unexplored passages;
- interesting formations;
- passages containing water;
- low areas;
- major chambers.

A sub-team must remain at the entrance throughout the exercise, keeping a log of movements and discoveries.

You must operate in groups of at least 3 at all times. Safety rules (attached) must be strictly observed.

Equipment

- ☐ helmets
- ☐ caving lamps
- ☐ boilersuits
- ☐ wellington boots
- ☐ first aid kit
- ☐ clip boards
- ☐ pencils and paper
- ☐ tea-making facilities.

42. MINE OF INFORMATION

Facilitator notes

Mine of Information is an absorbing project-based task requiring teamwork, coordination (often of remote teams), and creativity. There is a major element of non-underground work. In detail, the group's task is to make a presentation which contains a survey of a metal mine, together with historical notes, samples of ore products of the metal mining industry, a description of the miners' living conditions, and a history of the industry in the locality concerned.

Numbers 10 to 16.

Time 4 hours 30 minutes plus presentation time (say 20 minutes).

Equipment Caving and safety equipment should be provided by safety staff, and should be sufficient to allow a minimum of 8 delegates to be underground at any one time. At the very minimum, approved helmets and lamps (miners' lamps with traditional or nickel/cadmium batteries, *not* torches) should be provided, together with boilersuits and wellingtons. There should be ample backup lighting, which can include torches. In addition you should provide:

For the task

- ☐ a notebook and pen/pencil for each delegate
- ☐ sturdy plastic bags to protect notes underground
- ☐ hot drinks and packed lunch for all
- ☐ a plan of the mine and written material on the relevant industry, if available
- ☐ group-managed (staff-driven) transport.

For the presentation

- ☐ a flipchart and pens
- ☐ an overhead projector, viewfoils and pens.

Procedure Brief the group or leader at base, handing over equipment and written material, together with a list of locations. From then on it's up to them.

Prior training Can vary from none at all through to a full input on research methods and presentation skills. As a minimum, we suggest a short input and demonstration from technical staff on underground safety and the use of equipment.

Safety See pages 50–53 and issue Group Notes on safety in underground exercises.

Set-up

Location Although the exercise is limited to metal-mining areas, there are a surprising number of these. See the section dealing with underground activities (pages 27–28) for details. Coal-mining areas should only be used if a show-mine is at hand, as abandoned coal mines are extremely dangerous places.

Many areas also have show-mines or museums dedicated to mining. Even those without such facilities have libraries and general museums containing much relevant information.

The caving guides which are published for all caving areas sometimes also contain details of mines, but skilled local technical trainers are the best guides.

Once sites have been identified and access agreed, setting up is a matter of ensuring that the group is accompanied by safety tutors, is well equipped, and has the right materials.

Variations There are many variations for this exercise, mainly depending on what resources are available in the area. Although written for mines, with research it can be tailored to almost any industry. The most extreme use that we have made of it so far is for trainee butchers, who visited a farm, an abattoir, and a wholesale meat distributor.

GROUP NOTES

Mine of information

The task is quite comprehensive but the objective is clear: to make a presentation on the metal mining industry in this area. The presentation must be:

- interesting as far as content is concerned (suitable for giving to interested tourists, etc.);
- full of flair as far as presentation techniques are concerned. 'Flip and talk' is *not* what we (the customers!) want. Give us excitement, give us novelty, give us *entertainment*, take a few risks (in the presentation, that is)!
- factually true.

The presentation *must* contain a survey of an actual metal mine. Technical/safety staff may have some suggestions for suitable local mines. By 'survey' we mean an accurate map of the mine with profiles of key areas and calculations of the volume of any larger caverns. In order to conduct a survey, delegates going underground should have clearly defined jobs (measurer, recorder, etc.).

Any underground visit *must* be accompanied by technical staff in a ratio of 1:4 or better, and is limited to a maximum of 8 other people at any one time. Technical staff's rulings on safety matters are to be obeyed at all times when preparing to go underground, whilst underground, and when clearing up afterwards.

Technical staff will be glad to transport you to a suitable mine.

Useful information As accompanying information to this brief, we have enclosed a variety of useful and interesting written items on metal mining. Local museums and libraries are valuable sources of historical and background information. On request, members of staff will tell you the whereabouts of these.

Equipment Underground exploration and safety equipment is available from safety staff, and should be sufficient to allow 8 delegates to be underground at any one time. In addition, we have provided:

For the task

- ☐ a notebook and pen/pencil for each delegate
- ☐ sturdy plastic bags to protect notes underground
- ☐ hot drinks and packed lunch for all
- ☐ written material on the relevant industry
- ☐ transport (managed by you, driven by staff).

For the presentation

- ☐ a flipchart and pens
- ☐ an overhead projector, viewfoils and pens
- ☐ your own imagination.

Time allowed 4 hours 30 minutes plus presentation time (aim for between 15 minutes and a maximum of 20 minutes).

Safety Detailed notes are attached. Be sure that you read and understand these.

43. THE RESCUERS DOWN UNDER

Facilitator notes

This activity is challenging, exciting and demanding. You must choose a cave that is well mapped and known to your safety staff and suitable in terms of safety and ecology for the task envisaged. As with all such activities it is important to provide a role for those who prefer not to go underground, such as the tea-making role detailed in the group notes. It is not necessary to pretend the rescue is real to get the learning from the exercise; indeed, if not wholly convincing, such pretence can detract from the exercise.

Numbers 8 to 12.

Time 1–2 hours.

Materials

For the 'casualty'

- ☐ sleeping bag
- ☐ survival bag
- ☐ flask of hot drink.

For the group

- ☐ caving helmets
- ☐ caving lamps
- ☐ boilersuits
- ☐ wellington boots
- ☐ first aid kit

- ☐ stretcher
- ☐ tea-making facilities (not flasks).

Set-up A casualty needs to be pre-positioned in the cave. This needs to be someone well qualified and competent to cave alone or otherwise should be escorted into the location.

Procedure This task benefits from a verbal brief, adding immediacy and realism to the scenario.

Safety Normal cave safety rules apply, including staff ratios. Issue Group Notes on safety underground (see pages 50–53). Take particular care when the 'casualty' is being moved.

GROUP NOTES

The rescuers down under

A caver has just returned from _______________ cave and reported that a colleague has fallen and cannot get out. The local cave rescue team is already involved at another incident and you have been asked to assist.

You are to find the injured caver and, if possible, bring him/her out of the cave and down to the nearest road.

You are to leave a sub-team at the surface to coordinate your search, liaise with the cave rescue team on arrival and prepare a hot drink for the casualty and rescue party.

Equipment

- ☐ helmets
- ☐ caving lamps
- ☐ boilersuits
- ☐ wellington boots
- ☐ first aid kit
- ☐ stretcher
- ☐ tea-making facilities.

You must operate in groups of at least 3 at all times. Safety rules (attached) must be strictly observed.

44. The tube

Facilitator notes

The Tube is a project-based task in which the group conducts a survey of a cave with the objective of producing a map of the cave and means of access to it.

Numbers 10 to 16.

Time 4 hours 30 minutes, plus actual presentation time (say 15 minutes) and travel.

Equipment Caving and safety equipment should be provided by safety staff, and should be sufficient to allow a minimum of 8 delegates to be underground at any one time. At the very minimum, approved helmets and lamps (miners' lamps with traditional or nickel/cadmium batteries, *not* torches) should be provided, together with boilersuits and wellingtons. There should be ample backup lighting, which may include torches. In addition you should provide:

For the survey

- ☐ a notebook and pen/pencil for each delegate
- ☐ sturdy plastic bags to protect notes underground
- ☐ 3 × surveyors' measuring tapes
- ☐ 3 × Silva or similar compasses
- ☐ 2 × clinometers (simple and inexpensive ones are available from educational suppliers)
- ☐ a 'tube map'-quality plan of the cave, copied (but if necessary simplified) from the relevant cave guidebook
- ☐ hot drinks and energy food (chocolate, etc.) for all.

For the presentation

- ☐ a flip chart and pens
- ☐ an overhead projector, viewfoils and pens.

Procedure To avoid distractions, brief the leader or group at a place away from the cave entrance. Once the brief has been issued, it's over to them. The exercise concludes with a presentation of the survey findings to the course staff or, if feasible, an audience of local cavers or dignitaries. Allow time for cleaning up before reviewing.

Prior training Can vary from none at all (but with group access to written notes on cave surveying techniques) right through to the group having practised cave surveying in a cellar or similar environment. We suggest a short input from technical/safety staff on safety and the use of the equipment as the minimum prior training.

Variations With centres that specialize in caving, this exercise can be expanded and extended, but we have found that it palls after the time which we have suggested. An interesting variant is to have groups calculate the *volume* of air in the cave.

Safety See notes on safety in underground exercises on pages 50–53 and issue Group Notes on safety.

Set-up Although the exercise is largely confined to limestone areas, most of these have a semi-acknowledged beginners' cave in which it is best to carry out this task. The caving guides which are published for all caving areas are useful, but skilled local technical trainers are the best guides.

Once sites have been identified and access agreed, setting up is a matter of ensuring that the group is accompanied by safety tutors, is well equipped, and has the right materials.

GROUP NOTES

The tube

The task A project in which you conduct a survey, with the objective of producing a map of a cave and the means of access to it, and making a presentation of your findings to an audience supplied by course staff. Details of this task are as follows:

1. Produce a detailed map of as much of the cave as possible. This map should be sufficiently detailed to show variations in the width of passages, side-passages, and any areas of interest, such as striking rock-formations, 'squeezes', 'crawls' and so on. Notes to the map should include a minimum of 3 accurate drawings of sections of the cave, with measurements shown. These drawings should be as varied as possible. The objective for this part is accuracy. Quality is more important than quantity.
2. Produce a side-view of the area you have mapped in detail. This should also be as accurate as possible, showing the gradient of the cave and roof heights.
3. Produce an outline map of as much of the cave as safety staff will allow you to visit. In this case, detail is less important but junctions, squeezes, caverns, and other really prominent features should be shown.
4. Produce a map of how to reach the cave from the nearest point of vehicular access. This map should show gradients and points of interest along the way. It should be accurate and interesting.

On request, safety staff will conduct you to the cave entrance.

Equipment

For the survey

- ☐ caving and safety equipment to allow a minimum of 8 delegates to be underground at any one time
- ☐ a notebook and pen/pencil for each delegate
- ☐ sturdy plastic bags to protect notes underground
- ☐ 3 × surveyors' measuring tapes
- ☐ 3 × Silva or similar compasses
- ☐ 2 × clinometers
- ☐ a 'tube map'-quality plan of the cave
- ☐ hot drinks and energy food (chocolate, etc.) for all.

For the presentation (back at base)

- ☐ a flipchart and pens
- ☐ an overhead projector, viewfoils and pens.

Maximum time allowed 4 hours 30 minutes, plus travel to the centre and 15 minutes (max.) presentation time.

Safety Detailed notes are attached. Be sure you read and understand these.

CHAPTER 11

Combined exercises

45. Free transfer

Facilitator notes

Although this exercise is time consuming it provides some very useful learning opportunities and links well into other exercises. It can be used on a long course to simulate functional roles within an organization, e.g. replacing finance, production and distribution with climbing, navigating and water skills. The delegates are initially taught their skills and then, in an exercise requiring careful planning, coordination and excellent communication, they give each of their colleagues a taste of their newly acquired skill.

A location is required where all three activities can be practised within reasonable travelling distance. Navigation can be done almost anywhere, but canoeing and climbing require specific locations. The training should be done at three distinct locations, but scope allowed for delegates to choose to use only two in the activity phase, thus easing the logistics of the exercise.

Numbers 12 to 20.

Time 4–6 hours.

Materials

- ☐ climbing equipment
- ☐ canoes and associated equipment
- ☐ maps, romers and compasses.

Procedure

1. Brief team.
2. Conduct training sessions.
3. Monitor planning session.
4. Supervise activities.

Prior training Training sessions by properly qualified instructors as part of the exercise:

- *Climbing* – Teach delegates how to rig and supervise a short climb and abseil.
- *Navigation* – Teach delegates how to read and plot grid references and bearings.
- *Canoeing* – Teach delegates how to launch, paddle, steer, and right a canoe.

Variations Substitute different skills.

Safety All training sessions should include comprehensive safety briefs, then delegates should be made responsible for safety, but closely monitored.

GROUP NOTES

Free transfer

Objectives

1. To learn a new skill.
2. To introduce somebody else to this skill.

Phase 1 In 3 groups you will be trained in Climbing, Map Reading and Canoeing.

Phase 2 You will plan and carry out the following:

- At least 50% of the team members who have no prior climbing experience to complete a short climb and abseil at ________________ . This activity to be witnessed by safety staff.
- All team members to be taught how to plot 6-figure grid references and take a bearing. Training staff may test some delegates.
- At least 50% of team members with no prior canoeing experience to negotiate a short canoe course at __________________________ . This activity to be witnessed by safety staff.

Resources

- ☐ All necessary equipment for the activities will be provided
- ☐ 2 vehicles to transport between locations
- ☐ packed lunches.

Safety

- All safety rules must be strictly observed.
- The safety staff will not assist, but will monitor safety and intervene to correct unsafe practices.
- The vehicles can only be driven by our staff.
- No activity is to take place without staff safety supervision.

Timings

0900–1030 – training sessions.
1030–1130 – planning.
1130–1500 – activities.
1530–1630 – review.

46. Get smart!

Facilitator notes

Get Smart! is an exercise which combines the tasks *Twin Peaks, Triple Barrel* and *Container Ferry* (under different names) into an absorbing and challenging larger exercise.

Numbers 5 to 18. (The exercise can be run simultaneously with 3 groups of up to 6, provided 3 staff are available.)

Time Allow 90 minutes.

Equipment As for exercises *Twin Peaks, Triple Barrel* and *Container Ferry*.

Procedure The notes which follow assume a 3-group exercise. Modify accordingly if you are working in 1 or 2 groups.

1. **Set-up** the tasks so that they are out of sight and meaningful sound of each other. Synchronize watches with your fellow trainers and agree the order in which groups are to carry out the phases of the exercise, and an appropriate transit-time between exercises.
2. After separating the group into its three components, each trainer should take his or her team to the relevant start-point and issue either the group or the leader with the overall brief, and the brief for the relevant phase. Thereafter, it's over to them.
3. At the end of the first phase, announce that time is up, rotate to the next phase and issue the brief for it. Repeat the procedure, close, and review.

4. If a group completes a phase very quickly, you may need to hold a short interim review to stay in synchronization with other teams.

Prior training None required.

Safety As for each task brief.

GROUP NOTES

Get Smart!

OVERALL BRIEF

Background Maxwell Smart, an eccentric millionaire, has decided to set up a team to rescue people from the clutches of the various extremist and criminal groups around the world which indulge in the sport of hostage-taking.

He has set up various tests to simulate situations in which such a team might find itself, but is unsure as to whether these are appropriate. He therefore wishes you to try them out and report back on ways in which the tests were useful in helping you work as a team, and ways in which they 'stretched' you. He would also like to know what factors of teamwork were highlighted by the task.

You have 3 tests to try out. In each case you will be given twenty minutes to attempt the task involved; and you have five minutes to digest *this* brief.

Maxwell Smart has intimated that he will reward successful teams in a tangible form.

Good luck – the first phase starts in five minutes' time.

GROUP NOTES

Crossing the swamp

Task Your group is to cross the area you see laid out before you. The area represents a noxious swamp, such as those found in areas where oil wells have been allowed to gush their precious black gold into the desert. In such a swamp it has been found that oil drums will stay on the surface, whilst planks and people will sink without trace. Thus, you have to cross the swamp with only the oil drums touching the ground. Any team member or plank touching the ground will be deemed to have been swallowed up forever by the oily morass.

Materials

- ☐ 3 × 45-gallon drums
- ☐ 2 × 2m (7ft) wooden planks
- ☐ climbing helmets for each group member
- ☐ gardening gloves for each group member.

You may not supplement this equipment.

Time allowed 20 minutes.

Safety rules are as follows:

- Tutors' rulings on matters of safety are final and binding.
- No one may jump from any structure you build.
- Helmets and gloves will be worn.
- You must be aware of the need for safe working practices at all times.

GROUP NOTES

Tower block

Often, hostage-takers work in urban environments. This task is designed to test potential rescue-team members' abilities to cope in such a situation. In effect, your task is to get from A to B, as indicated by the tutor. Neither you nor any of your equipment must touch the ground or the tree.

The start point A and finishing point B represent the flat roof of a tower block, the drums represent the concrete pillars of an unfinished building, and the hanging tyre the jib of a crane.

Equipment

- ☐ 1 × plank
- ☐ 1 × rope
- ☐ helmets
- ☐ gloves.

You have 20 minutes.

GROUP NOTES

Beat the lock

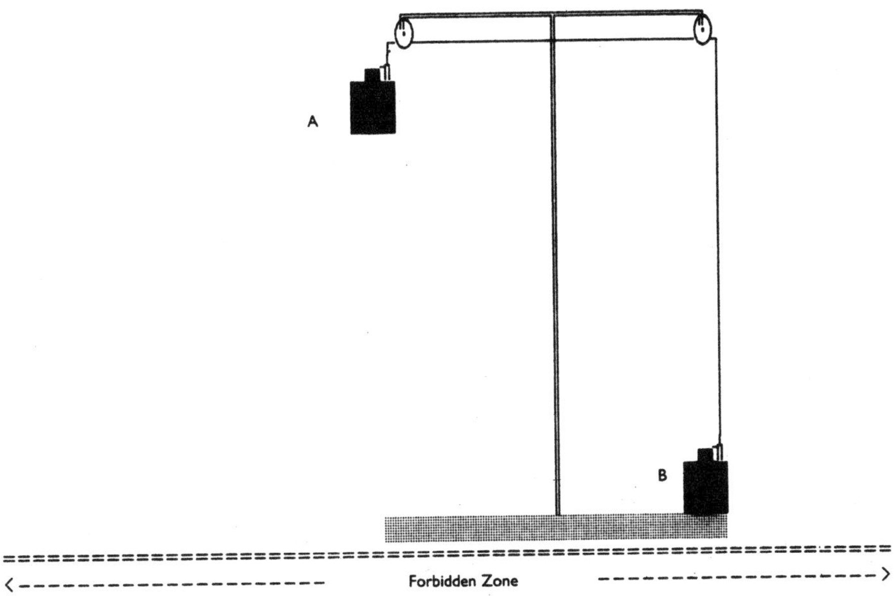

Diagram not to scale

Rescue teams often have to deal with fiendishly difficult unlocking mechanisms. The device which you see before you and which is illustrated above represents such a one. In effect, by changing the balance of the containers so that container A touches the ground and container B is up in the air, you defuse a particularly nasty minefield through which you wish to travel.

The extent of the minefield is shown as a rope circle on the ground and in the diagram as the Forbidden Zone. For anything to touch the ground in this area would mean almost certain and unpleasant death. The structure to which the mechanism is attached is also booby-trapped, so once again, if anything touches this, you have failed.

Only the equipment provided may be used. To avoid leaving evidence of your passing, equipment may not be wilfully defaced or damaged.

Resources

- ☐ 1 × 1.20m (4ft) plastic drainpipe
- ☐ 1 × 0.85m (3ft) plastic drainpipe
- ☐ 3 × plastic mugs
- ☐ 1 × full reel masking tape
- ☐ 1 × 4.20m (14ft) 5mm polypropylene rope
- ☐ 1 large bucket of water.

Time 20 minutes.

Safety If any lifting of heavy weights is required, consult with your trainer for correct methods before proceeding. You must apply safe working practices at all times.

47. JACK AND JILL OF ALL TRADES

Facilitator notes

This major exercise lends itself to a lot of customization in learning outcomes and content. The delegates plan and execute a large number of tasks over a period of time in a simulation of a small company performing contracts. There are financial elements, resource constraints and abundant potential for lessons in managing people.

Many of the exercises in this sourcebook can be included, but some should be customized to the locality. Tasks marked * in the list given on page 238 are stand-alone tasks, for which full briefs, equipment lists, etc., have already been given in this book. Details of all the other tasks, including lists of equipment and relevant safety notes, are given in the appendix, 'Supplementary Exercises'.

The timings are important, but very flexible. The exercise is in three distinct phases, the planning, the execution and the review. The learning outcomes will play an important part in the balance between these, but beware of allowing too little time for any phase.

The planning will take a surprisingly large amount of time (at least one and a half hours), but will invariably prove Parkinson's law that work expands to fill the time allotted. It may be advisable to allow a reasonable buffer between planning and the execution phase, but beware of spending too much time on it. Planning can usefully be done the night before the execution phase, but this may mean people working very late and to little avail.

The execution phase should allow enough time to complete a reasonable number of the tasks with a time allowance for reviews. Anything from 6 to 8 hours is reasonable. Such a time-scale brings extra planning considerations into play, such as meals. Depending on learning outcomes and the flexibility of the meals provider, you can legislate for this or leave delegates to plan it in appropriately. If you choose the latter, ensure that delegates make arrangements for feeding the staff, or you may go hungry!

The review phase is obviously the most crucial and should be given enough time and attention. It will require at least 2 hours to review all the learning properly. The success of this phase depends partly on the amount and depth of mini-reviews conducted during the execution phase. If these are neglected, important learning will be lost or devalued.

Variations

- Make all tasks compulsory.
- Impose extra compulsory tasks during the planning or execution phases, to examine management of change.
- Run for 2 or more teams in competition – they will need to collaborate on use of equipment and staff.

Numbers 6 to 20.

Time 10–12 hours.

Task list

Ball race
*Blind intent**
Child's play
*Cook's tour**
Corks!!!
An eggscruciating task
Exercise review
The game of the name
Jugglers
Kite
Lego tractor
The man who came in from the code
Mini-quiz
On yer bike
Paper aeroplane
Pressers
Signal success
Skippers
Stretchers
Sweet charity
Towering infernal
*Up Pompeii**

Materials

- ☐ A1 paper (Flip Chart)
- ☐ A4 paper
- ☐ abseil kit, complete, including harnesses
- ☐ art materials
- ☐ blindfolds
- ☐ bucket
- ☐ climbing kit, complete, including harnesses
- ☐ climbing helmets
- ☐ a coded message (and solution!)
- ☐ compasses
- ☐ cycle helmets
- ☐ empty milk bottle
- ☐ empty wine bottle with cork inside
- ☐ hard boiled eggs
- ☐ Lego Technic model kit
- ☐ List of Cook's Tour questions
- ☐ local climbing guidebook
- ☐ map reading instruction
- ☐ maps
- ☐ model building materials, such as balsa wood, dowel etc.
- ☐ mountain bike(s)
- ☐ plank
- ☐ 2 × 30m (100ft) ropes
- ☐ rulers, 12-inch
- ☐ Sellotape
- ☐ skipping rope
- ☐ stopwatch
- ☐ string, balls of
- ☐ surveyor's tape-measure
- ☐ tennis balls × 6
- ☐ tent
- ☐ torches
- ☐ whistles.

Set-up

- *Jack of all trades* itself needs little set-up apart from assembling the equipment, although some of the suggested component tasks require some.
- *The man who came in from the code* requires the preparation of a coded message. A code can be invented or taken from a code book, which can be found in libraries or bookshops. Children's encyclopedia are a good source.
- *Lego tractor* requires the purchase of a model from the 'Lego Technic' range, not necessarily a tractor.
- *Ball race* involves laying out, with string or tape, a 10m (30ft) circle and a throwing-line about 20m (60ft) away.
- *Signal success* requires the preparation of a suitable 5-word message or phrase. Some long or complex words add to the challenge, as do corruptions of well known slogans or proverbs.
- *Mini-quiz* needs newspapers. Resourcing these can be left to the

delegates, or they can be provided, which allows the use of older copies and easier access to the answers!

- *On yer bike* requires the planning and preparation of a course. This should not be too long or difficult as most of the delegates will not be accomplished mountain cyclists, but nor should it be too easy, as this may disappoint. Identify and mark one or two areas where feet may not touch down. It is useful to attempt the course yourself to test its difficulty and the time required to complete a run.
- *Cook's Tour* requires setting up as explained in the separate brief.
- *Up Pompeii* requires setting up as explained in the separate brief.

Procedure

1. Brief the exercise and answer any questions about the process and logistics. Thereafter monitor the planning session, answering appropriate questions and giving advice where necessary. Beware of solving problems for the teams, and discourage them from trying to solve task problems or actually do tasks at this stage, as opposed to simply identifying the problems and planning how to approach them.
2. During the execution phase it is vital that someone acts as exercise coordinator, keeping track of groups, safety staff and equipment. This also allows a very good opportunity to observe process and help identify learning points. All staff should encourage and monitor review sessions after each task, or at any other time deemed appropriate.
3. During the review phase allow the groups to draw their own conclusions but be prepared to assist and remind them of pertinent incidents and observations. Chair the presentations and ensuing discussions.

GROUP NOTES

Jack and Jill of all trades

INTRODUCTION

This exercise is designed to practice leadership, teamwork and communications.

The exercise is in 3 phases: planning, execution and review. The first phase enables you to plan how to tackle a number of tasks successfully within the given constraints. The tasks are outlined on the separate task sheets.

Some of the tasks are *compulsory* and must be attempted by the team. More of the tasks are *supplementary* and are entirely optional. The remainder are *choice* tasks and you *must* attempt 3 of these.

PHASE 1 – PLANNING AND INSPECTION

During this phase, you are to plan how you will complete the tasks in the allotted time and within the constraints. All team members should assemble to present your plans when ready, by ______________ at the latest, to the tutors for approval. Plans should include outline timings and profit projections.

You may also inspect some of the tasks or their venue. Those you are allowed to inspect are indicated on the task sheets. Try to avoid looking for solutions at this stage, just identify the problems.

Planning considerations

- There are 2 safety staff available for tasks requiring their assistance.
- There are 2 vehicles available, with your own drivers.
- Equipment is available as detailed in the attached price list.
- Costs should be offset against your expected earnings, each task being worth a number of points for successful completion, as indicated on the task sheets.
- Throughout the planning phase questions to the tutor will be answered free of charge.
- Maps and equipment may be borrowed at no cost, but must be returned by ________________ , when you present your plans.

Learning opportunities

In an exercise of this type learning opportunities are many and varied. Remember your personal learning outcome and look to advance it. Each team member should find at least one opportunity to act in a leadership role and will be expected to talk about this in the review. You should spend at least 10 minutes reviewing each task on completion.

PHASE 2 – THE TASK COMPLETION

From ___________ until ___________ you will attempt the tasks, according to your plan. Amendments to the plan may be necessary to address unforeseen problems, but tutors will expect at least 15 minutes' notice of any change in their required involvement.

PHASE 3 – REVIEW

The team will divide into 3 sub-teams to review the learning from the exercise. You have 45 minutes from _____________ to consider the major learning points relating to leadership, teamwork and communications. Each sub-team will prepare to make a 10 minute presentation to the assembled course, highlighting group and individual learning points.

JACK AND JILL'S TASK LIST

Task		Task	
Ball Race	%	Mini-quiz	
Blind Intent	%	On yer Bike	* #
Child's Play	~	Paper Aeroplane	%
Cook's Tour	~	Pressers	%
Corks!!!		Signal Success	%
An Eggscruciating Task		Skippers	%
Exercise Review	~	Stretchers	%
The Game of the Name	~	Sweet Charity	
Jugglers	%	Towering Infernal	~
Kite	%	Up Pompeii	* #
Lego Tractor			
The Man who came in from the Code	~		

* = 'choice' task
\# = safety cover required
% = completion must be witnessed
~ = compulsory task

EXERCISE REVIEW

This task involves you in reviewing your performance during the exercise. You should spend some time doing this task at regular intervals throughout the exercise, but particularly between ____ and ____, at which time you will be required to present your findings and conclusions in a plenary session. You should consider:

- How well did you work as a team?
- What were your strengths and weaknesses, how did you deal with or utilize these?
- In what areas or processes did you improve during the exercise – how and why?
- What valuable lessons did you learn?
- What parallels did you recognize with your working environment?
- What changes do you propose to make back at work?
- Any other area or question that you feel is relevant or useful.

This task is, of course, the most vital of all, and you should not neglect it. Staff will be delighted to offer any help or advice.

Price list	**Points**
A1 paper	15
A4 paper	5
abseil kit	100
advice, useful	25
advice, useless	10
blindfolds	5
bucket	10
climbing kit	500
climbing helmet	30
compass	20
Cook's Tour Question Sheet	Free
cycle helmet	25
instruction	50
Lego kit	25
list	30
map-reading instruction	50
map	25
mountain bike	100
plank	10
rope, 30m	50
ruler	10
Sellotape	10
skipping-rope	20
string	10
tape-measure	25
tent	10
torch	50
whistle	10

Other items: price on request.

Task values	Points
Ball Race, 4 balls	100
Ball Race, 5 balls	150
Blind Intent in >20 minutes	750
Blind Intent in <20 minutes	1000
Blind Intent in <15 minutes	1500
Child's Play	up to 300
Cook's Tour	see separate brief
Corks!!!	50
An Eggscruciating Task	75
Exercise Review	
The Game of the Name	500
Jugglers, 3 balls	75
Jugglers, 4 balls	150
Jugglers, 5 balls	300
Kite	150
The Lego Tractor	300
The Man who came in from the Code	250
Mini-quiz	up to 100
On yer Bike	up to 300
Paper Aeroplane	100
Pressers, 3 people synchronized	300
Pressers, 2 people synchronized	100
Pressers, 1 person	20
Signal Success	60
Skippers, 3 people	325
Skippers, 2 people	125
Skippers, 1 person	25
Stretchers	210
Sweet Charity, per £1 earned	100
Towering Infernal	150
Up Pompeii	see separate brief

48. Monetary Multiplier

Facilitator notes

Monetary Multiplier is an exercise in which the group (or groups) gain points by performing as many tasks as possible from the list provided in Group Notes. There are some rules to make it a little more complicated:

- Groups must pay the stated purchase price of any task before they undertake it. Such payments are not returned if a group fails at a task.
- Groups pay rent, power, and rates at the rate of 50 points per hour.
- For those tasks requiring an element of performance (e.g. press-ups), a member of safety staff *must* be present.
- All costs and payments for the tasks are in points. At the end of the task these may be converted into real money at an appropriate rate of exchange.
- A task is not considered to be purchased by a group until they have presented you with a completed purchase voucher. Blank purchase vouchers should be issued to groups along with their briefing notes, and you should give payment vouchers for each task successfully completed ('blanks' attached).
- Each task may only be attempted once.
- Groups should keep accurate accounts and be able to display their financial situation to staff members at any time.

A list of tasks, values and costs is set out on page 251. Tasks marked * in the list are stand-alone tasks for which full briefs, equipment lists, etc., have already been given in this book. Details of the other tasks, including lists of equipment and relevant safety notes, are given in the appendix 'Supplementary Exercises'.

Time 7 hours.

Numbers As many teams of 6–8 as you require.

Materials See individual task briefs. In addition, a supply of paper, scissors, staples, string, coloured pens and pencils is useful.

Procedure Arrange for groups or leaders to be briefed separately, ensuring that they know where to find staff and equipment, and then it's over to them. Ensure that groups plan and enact reviews during the task as well as post-task.

At the close of the task phase it may be appropriate to gather groups together to announce final results before going into review.

Prior training None required.

Variations There are literally dozens of variations. The most popular are:

- Groups present accounts mid-exercise
- Equipment is hired at a prearranged cost
- A cash economy with 'funny money' is used instead of the voucher system, interest being charged on overdrawings
- A complex points/contracts system is applied, whereby points are exchanged for contracts awarded at various pre-set times. This variation means that points are merely raw stocks, which are then translated into income at a later date – perhaps a more realistic reflection of business life, especially if interest is charged on borrowing.

PURCHASE VOUCHER

Task: ______________________ Group: ______________________

Purchase price: ________points Time: ______________________

Signed ____________________________for group

= =

PURCHASE VOUCHER

Task: ______________________ Group: ______________________

Purchase price: ________points Time: ______________________

Signed ____________________________for group

= =

PURCHASE VOUCHER

Task: ______________________ Group: ______________________

Purchase price: ________points Time: ______________________

Signed ____________________________for group

= =

PURCHASE VOUCHER

Task: ______________________ Group: ______________________

Purchase price: ________points Time: ______________________

Signed ____________________________for group

= =

PAYMENT VOUCHER

Task: ____________________ Group: ____________________

This voucher is in payment for the above task,

and is valued at ______points. Time: ____________________

Signed ________________________for staff

= =

PAYMENT VOUCHER

Task: ____________________ Group: ____________________

This voucher is in payment for the above task,

and is valued at ______points. Time: ____________________

Signed ________________________for staff

= =

PAYMENT VOUCHER

Task: ____________________ Group: ____________________

This voucher is in payment for the above task,

and is valued at ______points. Time: ____________________

Signed ________________________for staff

= =

PAYMENT VOUCHER

Task: ____________________ Group: ____________________

This voucher is in payment for the above task,

and is valued at ______points. Time: ____________________

Signed ________________________for staff

= =

GROUP NOTES

Monetary multiplier

Monetary Multiplier is an exercise in which you gain points by performing as many tasks as possible from the list provided. Rules are:

- You must pay the stated purchase price of any task before you undertake it. Such payments are not returned if you fail at a task.
- You pay rent, power, and rates at the rate of 50 points per hour.
- For those tasks requiring an element of performance (e.g. press-ups), a member of safety staff *must* be present.
- All payments and costs for the tasks are in points. A supply of blank purchase vouchers is attached, and you will be given payment vouchers for each task successfully completed.
- Each task may only be attempted once.
- You should keep accurate accounts and be able to display your financial situation to staff members at any time.

A list of tasks, values and costs is attached.

Time 7 hours.

Materials See individual task briefs.

COMPONENT TASKS OF MONETARY MULTIPLIER

Task	Value (points)	Cost (points)
All Aloft*	50	20
Baker's Dozen	up to 300	120
Balsa Flier (per metre)	15	90
Blind Intent*	100	40
Child's Play	up to 300	100
Corks!!!	50	20
The Crate Escape*	150	60
Credibility Gap*	150	60
First Service* (per metre)	15	90
The Game of the Name	up to 150	60
Going the Distance* (per metre)	15	90
Humpty Dumpty	up to 300	60
Jugglers – 2 balls	50	120
3 balls	200	120
4 balls	300	120
5 balls	500	120
Lego Tractor	up to 400	150
Poacher's Escape*	150	60
Pressers – 3 people	300	80
2 people	100	80
1 person	20	80
Signal Success	80	30
Skippers – 3 people	325	100
2 people	125	100
1 person	25	100
Stretchers	100	40
Triple Barrel*	100	40
Upwardly Mobile	up to 200	80

APPENDIX I

SUPPLEMENTARY EXERCISES

GROUP NOTES

Baker's Dozen

Baker's Dozen is an exercise in resource investigation, in which you bake a cake sufficient to feed 12, and serve it with morning coffee or afternoon tea.

Value A member of staff will award points depending on:

- visual appeal of the cake (up to 40% of points);
- taste of the cake (up to 60% of points).

The cake *must* be baked by a member of the group, not delegated to an outsider or bought in.

Safety The usual kitchen hygiene and safety procedures apply.

GROUP NOTES

Ball Race

The task is to throw 4 out of 5 tennis-balls into a circle of rope so that the balls stop within the circle. Each ball may bounce only *once* before it enters the circle.

GROUP NOTES

Balsa Flier

Balsa Flier is a task in which you design and build a flying glider from balsa-wood.

The glider must be launched at ground level by means of an elastic band or by throwing, and must fly a course over approximately level ground.

Value depends on the distance flown on the best of 3 launches observed by a member of course staff.

Materials

☐ balsa-wood sheets and blocks
☐ craft knife (Use carefully.)
☐ balsa cement
☐ cutting board (Please use this for all cutting operations.)
☐ large, wide elastic band.

GROUP NOTES

Child's Play

Child's Play is a task in which you invent a game that can be played by children of any age range that you choose, up to 13 years. The game should work for 2 players but also be playable by 4 or more.

There are 3 broad categories from which to choose:

- activity games (*Hide and Seek* is an example);
- board games (*Ludo* is an example);
- combination of board and activity games (role-playing games are an example).

Value depends on the following:

- originality (up to 30% of points);
- depth and quality of preparation (up to 30% of points);
- potential for enjoyment (up to 40% of points).

A demonstration game must be played in the presence of a member of course staff, who will judge it.

Materials Nothing specific is provided; use your 'resource investigation' skills.

GROUP NOTES

Corks!!!

Corks!!! requires you to remove a cork intact from inside a wine-bottle provided by course staff.

Materials One wine-bottle with cork inside it, and anything else you can find.

Safety The task does not require knives or fire, and so these should not be used.

GROUP NOTES

An eggscruciating task

Get a hard-boiled but shelled egg into a milk bottle without damaging the egg.

GROUP NOTES

The Game of the Name

The Game of the Name is a task in which you agree upon an appropriate name for your group and display it on the Group Room door, along with a logo which sums up the group's aims and objectives.

Value Staff will award points depending on:

- quality of artwork (up to 50% of points);
- appropriateness of the logo (up to 50% of points).

Materials Nothing specific is provided; use your 'resource investigation' skills.

GROUP NOTES

Humpty Dumpty

Humpty Dumpty requires you to drop an uncooked hen's egg from a second-floor window to the *ground* without that egg breaking. No one may stand within a horizontal radius of 4m around the egg's landing-site.

Performance must be observed by a member of staff, who will show you the window in question.

Materials

- ☐ one uncooked hen's egg
- ☐ up to 20 sheets plain A4 paper
- ☐ up to 3m sticky tape
- ☐ up to 20 drinking-straws
- ☐ adhesive 'tac-putty'.

Housekeeping Group members must ensure that no members of the public are at risk from falling eggs, and must clear up after egg-dropping.

GROUP NOTES

Jugglers

Jugglers is a task in which you earn points by juggling tennis-balls for 20 seconds without dropping them. Performance must be observed by a member of staff.

Value depends on the number of balls juggled (between 2 and 5).

Materials 5 tennis-balls.

GROUP NOTES

Kite

Make and fly a kite capable of carrying a table-tennis ball to a height of 15m.

GROUP NOTES

Lego Tractor

Lego Tractor is a straightforward task: to build a tractor from the Lego parts provided. The tractor *must* conform as far as possible to the instructions provided.

Value depends on accuracy in conforming to instructions, completeness, and quality of workpersonship.

Materials One Lego Technics tractor kit and instructions.

GROUP NOTES

The Man who came in from the Code

Your task is to decode a message, available from the exercise director on request during the execution phase only.

GROUP NOTES

Mini-quiz

Correctly complete a crossword from today's newspaper.

Independent:	100% of available points
Times:	80% of available points
Daily Telegraph:	60% of available points
D.T. Quick:	40% of available points
Express:	20% of available points

GROUP NOTES

On yer bike!

Basically, the task is a mountain-bike time-trial event. Your score depends on your speed and dexterity in negotiating the course. A penalty of 10 seconds will be incurred for a foot touching the ground in areas where this is not allowed.

Scoring

Fastest computed time:	25% of points available.
Second fastest time:	20% of points available.
Third fastest time:	15% of points available.
Fourth fastest time:	13% of points available.
Fifth fastest time:	11% of points available.
Sixth fastest time:	9% of points available.
Seventh fastest time:	7% of points available.

Safety You must wear the protective clothing provided, and obey any safety instructions from the staff member on site.

GROUP NOTES

Paper Aeroplane

Make a paper aeroplane and fly it continuously for 12 seconds. The plane is to be made entirely from paper and launched from ground level.

GROUP NOTES

Pressers

In *Pressers* you earn points by completing 15 press-ups in one session, with no rests. Performance and practice for this task must be observed by a member of safety staff.

Value varies according to the number of people who accomplish the task. If 2 or more people are performing concurrently, the press-ups must be synchronized.

Safety This task is not suitable for group members who suffer from heart, lung, or other internal conditions, or back problems, or who are overweight. It requires a good level of fitness for successful completion.

For health reasons, women participating in the task should do press-ups from the knees, not the toes.

GROUP NOTES

Signal Success

In *Signal Success* you transmit a 5-word message (given to the transmitter at the appropriate time by a member of staff) by visual means across a space of 100m without using voice or written words/letters. Performance must be observed by a member of staff who will conduct the transmitter to his/her place on request.

Equipment Nothing specific is provided; use your 'resource investigation' skills.

GROUP NOTES

Skippers

Skippers is a task in which you earn points by skipping 100 times *with one rope*. You are allowed 3 breaks, but apart from these must not interrupt the skipping sequence.

Breaks must be pre-planned, and should be notified to a member of staff before you start skipping. Performance and practice for this task must be observed by a member of safety staff.

Value depends on number of people (1 to 3) concurrently skipping with one rope only.

Equipment One long skipping rope.

Safety This task is not suitable for group members with health restrictions such as heart or lung conditions, or who are overweight, and requires a good level of fitness for successful completion.

GROUP NOTES

Stretchers

Stretchers requires you, using only one 30m (100ft) rope, to build a stretcher and carry any delegate 50 metres in it without dropping them and without the stretcher failing. Performance and practice for this task must be observed by a member of safety staff.

Materials One 30m length of 10mm polypropylene rope.

Safety The task of carrying the stretcher is not suitable for group members with health restrictions such as backache or heart or lung conditions, and requires a reasonable level of fitness for successful completion.

GROUP NOTES

Sweet Charity

Earn some money for a charity, within the following constraints:

- Money must be earned, not begged.
- You may not take money from course staff, delegates or hotel staff.
- You must not make nuisances of yourselves.
- Whatever you do must be legal!
- Earnings depend on money donated (after costs).

GROUP NOTES

Towering Infernal

Determine, from ground level only, the highest point of the building as defined by a member of the course staff.

GROUP NOTES

Upwardly mobile

Upwardly mobile requires you to create a mobile suitable for hanging in clients' premises to advertise your product or service.

Value Staff will award points based on:

- mechanical soundness/complexity –is it mobile? are there variations in lengths and structures? (Up to 20% of points);
- originality and quality of materials and workpersonship (up to 30% of points);
- clarity of message (up to 20% of points);
- attractiveness (up to 30% of points).

Materials You may use your 'resource investigation' skills to supplement the following which are provided:

- ☐ metal coat-hangers (4)
- ☐ cotton or nylon thread –one reel
- ☐ scissors.

APPENDIX II

SUPPLEMENTARY NOTES

A BASIC REVIEW PROCESS

There are two extremes when reviewing. The first is for the trainer to be present acting as conductor of the review and 'pulling' the learning from the group, rather like a dentist drawing teeth. The other is the style in which the trainer allows the group a great deal of space, encouraging them to reflect individually and jointly on how they performed without necessarily sharing what they have learned with the trainer or other groups.

In our view a mix of the two approaches is usually more effective than exclusively employing either extreme. There are many other ways to review, and in discovering your own preferred ways of reviewing we would merely share some advice which we have found useful. This is: *Trust the group ... Trust the process...*

Three of our favourite approaches are:

The free-form approach

- After the exercises each group member is given time to think about and record what went well in process terms, and what could have been done differently.
- When all have done this, record and discuss the individual answers in plenary session, probing for resolutions to change and parallels with work.
- Arising from the above, discuss and agree approaches to apply in the exercises that follow.

Focused questioning

- From your observations of the group at work, formulate three or four pertinent questions which will focus the group's thoughts on key learning areas.
- In sub-groups with an appropriate time frame and preferably in separate rooms, invite the delegates to consider those questions, and come to conclusions.
- On completion of their deliberations, each sub-group should prepare and deliver in plenary a short presentation of their findings.
- From these presentations and subsequent discussion, draw out the appropriate learning, emphasising common ground (which is surprisingly often present), but not ignoring or devaluing conflicting conclusions.

The open approach

We recommend that this approach should only be used with a process-mature group, probably towards the end of a programme.

- Invite the group, in the most open of terms, to review the foregoing exercise. Facilitate any ensuing discussions.

Whatever approach you adopt, bear in mind two things:

- No matter how carefully exercises have been designed to fit particular needs, groups will often learn other things from them. If this is so, then so be it. *Trust the group ... Trust the process.*
- Often groups take time to settle in to experiential processes, and seem merely to be toying with review. A moment of truth, however, usually occurs, after which learning is greatly enriched. Do not try to force the pace before this moment. *Trust the group ... Trust the process.*

Some well-proven general review questions

- Ask individuals to consider what went well, what they could consider doing differently, and what are their resolutions for the next task.

- Give some time for individual reflection and then ask the question, 'What were the key issues in this task?'
- Start a discussion of how they performed by asking the question, 'In what ways was this like/not like work?' This has the added advantage that groups relate their performance on the task back to work.
- Ask individuals to record their personal view as to what were the two most important process (not task) items that led to success/failure of the exercise. Once recorded, these can be shared and the resulting processes highlighted and discussion developed.
- Give the team a short input or reminder on the problem-solving cycle and then seek from them their views on where the team performed best, and where it was least effective.
- Ask individuals to record their personal 'highs' and 'lows' and 'whys'. Once recorded, these can be shared and the resulting processes highlighted and discussion developed.
- Ask the question, 'How did you go about generating solutions?' and respond to the responses.

BRAINSTORMING

Brainstorming is a term used to describe any method for creating ideas when normal inspiration fails. The method described below is one of our favourites, but there are many others –all equally valuable.

Step 1 Clearly define the problem. Ensure that everyone fully understands it.

Step 2 Tell everyone that in 15 minutes time they *all* have to come up with 3 solutions to the problem. All solutions will be listened to, and it doesn't matter if the solutions proposed are really stupid! The emphasis here is on *quantity, not quality*. Encourage them to work individually to think about their solutions –that way, you will access 'N' brains. If people 'pair up', you only access 'N/2' brains!

Step 3 Come back together and let everybody share their three ideas. There are some rules which *must* be observed at this stage:

- *No interruptions!* – People should be able to explain their ideas with no criticism whatsoever.
- The ideas should be recorded on a paper chart or chalk-board.
- The Chair should ensure that *everyone* is able to present their three ideas. Don't just stop at the first one that looks good! The role of the chair-person may well be to encourage those who are a little shy to present their ideas.

Step 4 Debate the 'menu' of solutions. You may be able to choose one obvious one right away, or may need to debate for some time. New ideas – sometimes combinations of two or already recorded – may arise during this discussion time. Record these as well, and discuss until a solution which all understand is accepted. The chairperson will need to act as referee during this stage, but we have found that there always comes a stage at which you can 'feel' group consensus.

Step 5 Put the agreed solution into action.

INTERPERSONAL PROCESS

People have needs other than the physical. They work better if these needs are being met. Needs consist of, among other things:

Inclusion

Healthy relationships depend on people being (and feeling) included in what's going on. It helps them to be (and feel) more secure. 'Including' behaviour by managers entails:

- ensuring people are actually being involved in meetings, social activities, and groups. Few people go to work just for the money. They feel isolated and powerless if excluded (The Forgotten Army, what's the use, no one ever talks to me...)
- using first names (when the situation allows). Even phone calls to complain are more effective when they start, 'My name is John Doe and I...' than when the first words are, 'My name is *Mr.* Jones and I...'
- informing people as much as possible about what's going on. Otherwise, whether or not the lack of information actually affects their task performance, they will feel excluded. Nature abhors a vacuum, and if people are starved of information they will make up their own
- gaining commitment to goals. This often makes the difference between success or failure in the task.

Control

People have a real need to be (and feel) in control of their own destinies. We can help this if we:

- Give people control of what they can do well. Help them to learn how to do it well. Demonstrate your confidence in them, don't just say the words...

- Praise work well done. Reward competence (at least with praise). Coach them in areas where they need to improve.
- Set clear standards for performance. This includes abiding by those standards ourselves, in effect 'role-modelling' them. People get confused and cynical if they are being told to abide by a set of standards by someone who doesn't.

Affection

- Openness encourages openness. An open relationship is a healthy one. The opposite (with suspicions of hidden agenda etc.) encourages cover-ups. Self-disclosure is a helpful route to openness ('I had the same trouble myself when . . .').
- Feelings matter. Acknowledge them (in self and others). Also acknowledge others' personal concerns ('How will this affect *me*?') because they are real, and won't go away . . .
- Be trustworthy and reliable. This encourages trust. Be realistic in this – some people are rogues.
- Give compliments and praise. Be generous in this, but don't devalue the language of praise. Compliments and praise are best when focused on *particular* actions or pieces of work well done. 'You've all done very well!' rarely sounds like praise, often like bull-shine. Demonstrate to people that you like them, if you do.

Delegating

Delegating helps people to feel included, to have control, and to be trusted (a key to affection).

A PROBLEM-SOLVING PROCESS

This is a step-by-step process, with two keys for successful completion: you must not move on to the next step until you have completed the one before; you review at every stage...

1. *Identify problem*

   - State and define the problem.
   - Is everyone clear about the issues?
   - Does everyone agree about the issues?

2. *Agree objective*

   - What is it that we are trying to do?
   - What are our constraints?
   - How can we measure progress (milestones)?
   - How will we know we have succeeded?
   - Is it worth achieving?

3. *Generate ideas*

   - Brainstorm.
   - Listen.
   - Don't dismiss!
   - Choose from a menu.

4. *Plan in detail*

   - Agree who does what.
   - Agree deadlines.
   - Agree resources needed.
   - Agree milestones.
   - Agree standards.

5. *Do it*

   - Check quality.
   - Check timings.
   - *Watch* what's going on!
   - Safety.
   - Deal with unforeseen problems.

6. *Follow-up*

   - How could we improve?
   - What can we learn for another time?

THE TEAM FORMATION PROCESS

Teams do not just spring into active and vibrant life. They tend to go through a process which at times is painful. The process can be split into four stages, as identified by Tuckman:

1. Forming: The team gets together. If people know each other at all, it is at a fairly shallow level, but their survival in the organization depends on working together, so the tendency is to avoid conflict and be nice to each other at all costs. Potential areas of conflict are glossed over, problem areas politely skirted around and treated as dangerous minefields. One of the casualties in this phase is honesty. Effectiveness is often another. Sadly, some teams never evolve past this stage.

2. *Storming:* The second phase is the reverse of the first, and perhaps a reaction to it. Instead of avoiding conflict at all costs, the frustrations of the first phase lead to a period of often painful honesty, with suppressed feelings being aired publicly, even inappropriately, and blame being placed haphazardly. If the team survive this phase (and many do not), the mud begins to settle and the team moves on to the next phase.

3. *Norming:* The storm blows over, and the survivors become aware of emerging behavioural norms and group standards. They know each other well enough to have a mature appreciation of each other's strengths and weaknesses. This stage leads to the final phase of the formation process.

4. *Performing:* Basically, being comfortable enough with team norms and each other, and knowing the task and its pitfalls well enough to have the security to get on with the job in hand. This stage is sometimes followed by a process of decline.

The four-stage process is quite closely related to the 'grief curve' well-known to those working with the bereaved, and linked to the concept of transition-stress in employment by Ralph Lewis and Chris Parker.* The terms used for the phases of this process seem to coincide quite neatly with the phases of the team-formation process:

	TEAM FORMATION STAGES	TRANSITION STAGES
1	Forming	Denial
2	Storming	Blame
3	Norming	Acceptance
4	Performing	Development

* Lewis, R and Parker, C (1981) 'Beyond the Peter Principle – managing successful transitions', *Journal of European Industrial Training*, 5, 6.

PROBLEM-DEFINITION WINDOW

The Williams/Creswick Window

		PROBLEM	
		Clear	Unclear
SOLUTION	Clear	1	2
	Unclear	3	4

The Williams/Creswick Window

Box 1 is the area of routine decision-making with little or no stress.

Box 2 is the area where the problem needs diagnosis, but where, once the problem has been clarified, a solution is fairly obvious.

Box 3 is where the problem is clear but there are a variety of solution from which to choose.

Box 4 is the area of ultimate ambiguity, where neither the problem nor possible solutions clearly present themselves. Managers often have to exist within this area these days.

Developed by Roy Williams and Chris Creswick in the late 1970s, the Williams/Creswick Window helps people examine problems in terms of levels of complexity.

Examples

Box 1: Routine stuff. Once we have spotted the problem, we know what the solution is. An example would be that when stocks are running low, there's usually a simple re-ordering procedure. The skill is in knowing the system.

Box 2: Life is not always simple, and we sometimes have to define our problems. An example would be if your car is not working very well. A mechanic spends some time diagnosing the fault and, having done so, knows very quickly what to do about it. The skill of Box 2 is *not* to move on to solutions until the problem is clearly identified.

Box 3: The reverse of Box 2. The problem is clear, but there are a variety of possible solutions. In the late eighties, many farmers wrestled with a Box 3 problem: what to do with land no longer needed for agricultural use. The problem was very clear. No one wanted their produce any more. But what to do with the land? There were many options – golf-course, fallow, riding school, fishing ponds, and so on. The skill of the Box 3 operator is deciding which is best. Once that is done, the rest is routine operating procedures.

Box 4: The area of maximum uncertainty and maximum insecurity. More and more of us work in this area, where both the problems and the solutions are unclear. A classic example is the small consulting firm which has to react quickly to unexpected new areas of business, networking with other firms, giving each other work, and generally keeping very much on its toes.

A more down-to-earth example is the local fire brigade, which has to be prepared to cope with everything from rescuing a kitten from a tree to dealing with major chemical fires. Coping with such ambiguities is no easy task, and there are no right or wrong answers. Box 4 life is not that simple. The trick is to bias organization towards flexibility, and the skill is to be able to make decisions quickly on incomplete (but as complete as possible) information, instead of waiting for all the evidence to be available –because by then it's too late.

MANAGEMENT STYLES

The Human Zoo

The way people set their priorities and act at work can be classified by reference to two sets of bipolar extremes, represented here in terms of 'the Human Zoo':

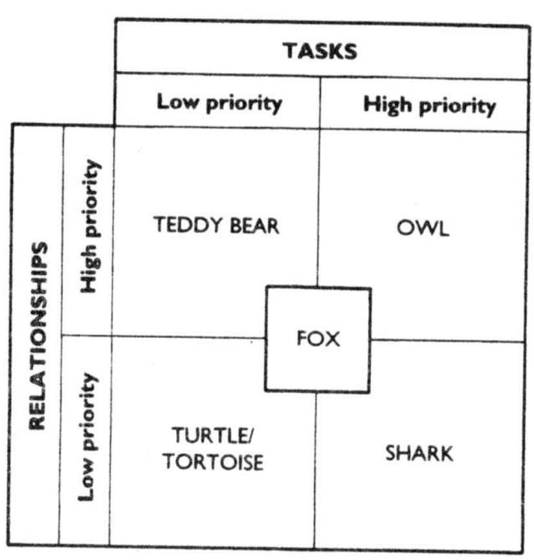

The Human Zoo (adapted by the authors from information provided by Simon Lovedoy)

The vertical axis refers to relationships. At the bottom of this axis, maintaining relationships with others is not important. At the top, building and maintaining relationships is all-important.

The horizontal axis is related to tasks and urgency of completion. Thus, at the bottom left the task is unimportant. At the top right the task and its completion are highly important.

There are four extreme positions and a central, compromise position. Each is appropriate at some time and in some situations, but most of us have a preference for one or another, which we may well use at both appropriate and inappropriate times.

1. *Teddy bear* (high relationship, low task): fine for being liked, and it is often useful to be liked. Difficult to maintain when in disagreement, and may lead to a 'flip' into the opposite mode. Can also, if overused, lead to too great submission to others.
2. *Turtle/tortoise* (low relationship, low task): 'turtle' because it involves withdrawal from both social *and* working life. Rarely appropriate, but we all know of times when it's best to keep our heads down! In extreme regimes, whether just at work or in general life, this is very much the survivor's position.
3. *Shark* (high task, low relationship): the job is paramount and relationships are at best irrelevant to the shark. If people stand in the way of the task, they are likely to be beaten down. Feelings will be brushed aside. Appropriate behaviour when something *must* be done urgently. Inappropriate when getting the job done involves the voluntary co-operation of others, as most jobs do.
4. *Owl* (high relationship, high task): in the 'owl' situation, relationships and the task have an equally high priority. This is often the best position to adopt in working life, and the most admired leaders tend to adopt it, but there are times when all the others –even the fifth, compromise, position –are useful and more appropriate to success, or at least survival.

   (We know of at least one owl who lost his very senior job because he failed to realize that the sharks were after blood. The turtles kept their heads down, the teddy bears accommodated, the foxes joined the sharks. He became isolated and was eventually forced into a position where the choice was resign or submit. He resigned.)
5. *Fox* (midway on relationships, midway on tasks): in effect this is a compromise position in which one indulges in give-and-take in relationships, and in tasks ('I'll help you only if you help me . . . I'll scratch your back if you scratch mine . . .'). Often used to pragmatically overcome deeply entrenched positions. Politicians often use foxiness to unravel such insoluble problems as Middle East peace. Human relations people (on both sides) sometimes need to adopt this position in solving industrial disputes. The danger of over-use is that one would be seen to be untrustworthy and pragmatic.

MAP READING NOTES

Sometimes people are put off by maps and think they can't read them. There are a number of reasons for this, including:

- Poor instruction in the past. As youths we were sometimes put off map reading through suffering under instructors who taught us very badly and then shouted at us when we didn't understand.
- Bad experiences with road maps. Most of us can recall times when roads have stubbornly refused to conform to the map. This is because road maps are to a very small scale and cannot show adequate detail. Some don't even have all village names on them!

Reading the 1:25,000 map

With the Ordnance Survey 1:25,000 scale map we recommend, things are relatively easy due to:

- Detail: the Ordnance Survey *Pathfinder* series 1:25,000 (i.e. about 2.5in. to the mile) scale, with editions available to cover the whole country, gives a very high degree of accuracy and detail, and is arguably the most reliable and detailed to that scale publicly available in the world.
- Consistency: the *Pathfinder* series is consistent in its scale, symbols and accuracy. This means that, given sufficient time and a systematic explanation, almost anyone can master it.

This section deals with the following areas:

- getting to know the map;
- common features including roads, bridleways and rights of way, water and hills;
- a technique for navigating in vehicles;
- 4-, 6- and 8-figure grid references: how to plot them, and their uses;
- common errors and how to avoid them.

To ensure you have understood the training, we include a short self-test exercise, based on a sample map included in the section. For technical reasons we are only able to include a black-and-white copy of the map, which is normally in colour. We therefore suggest you use a full-colour copy of a *Pathfinder* map appropriate to your area and, if instructing others, practice your own navigation skills on that beforehand.

We have rarely found compass work to be necessary for management programmes and have therefore not included a section on it. If it is necessary, numerous publications are available from the aforementioned sources and local outdoor shops.

Knowing the map

A useful feature of the map is the key. This explains all the symbols and abbreviations, and gives reminders on such things as public rights of way.

The scale of the map –1:25,000 – is about 2.5 inches per mile, which is twice as detailed as the more common 1:50,000 (about 1.25 inches to the mile) *Landranger* series. The latter are useful as very good local road and route maps, but lack sufficient space for great detail.

The map is covered with a printed grid. This is explained in detail later, but note that each grid square represents exactly one kilometre (about 5/8 of a mile). At 1:25,000 scale the size of each grid square on the map is 40mm, representing 1km squares. All Ordnance Survey maps in both the popular 1:25,000 and 1:50,000 scales have a kilometre grid.

Symbols

The most useful symbols are explained below:

Roads All roads maintained by local or national government for vehicular use are printed in various shades of reddish brown. The deeper the colour, the wider the print, the bigger the road.

A mixture of brown and white indicates a single-track road. A dotted or hatched margin to the road indicates that it is open to the countryside, *not* that it is particularly small.

Some roads are not maintained by local authorities and are shown on the map as two closely parallel black lines with a white space in between. These are private roads or tracks, and using them is in effect trespassing. Their condition varies from very good to totally undriveable. The map does not tell you which...

Public rights of way Shown as broken green lines. These are not necessarily public footpaths – there may not be a track or obvious path on the ground. The symbols merely indicate that the right to walk (not drive!) exists. Generally speaking, the more prominent the line, the more prominent the right of way. If the broken green lines are shaped approximately thus: ¬ they are bridleways on which horses and bicycles may also be ridden. Solid green lines indicate land owned by such organizations as the National Trust, upon which the right of open access can sometimes be presumed.

Contours Indicated by the brown, irregular lines. The height difference between lines is 5m. The tops of the printed numbers always point uphill. Most importantly, the closer the contours are together, the steeper the hill.

Water Areas of pale blue.

Buildings Grey shapes with a black edge.

Walls, fences, hedges Indicated by thin, unbroken black lines.

Ditches Thin, unbroken blue lines.

Woodland Areas of pale green, sometimes with pictures of the appropriate trees.

Team navigation (vehicles)

It is difficult for one person to navigate in a vehicle using a 1:25,000 map. This is because constant looking up and down leads to confusion and sometimes car sickness, and the map is on a large enough scale that it is easy to underestimate the distance travelled. Before you know it, a key turnoff has been passed.

It is therefore better to have navigators working in teams of two. One needs to be able to read the map, the other simply needs to be able to see and talk. The jobs work out like this:

Job 1: Map reader This job involves:

- taking charge of the map and ensuring that the position of the vehicle on the map is known at all times;
- listening to the information given by the observer;
- issuing navigation instructions to the driver.

Key skills:

- assertiveness
- map reading
- listening.

Job 2: Observer This job involves:

- observing fixed features (e.g. turnoffs, woodland, prominent buildings such as churches etc.) adjacent to the road, and observing general twists and turns of the road;
- reporting features promptly to the navigator. This usually takes the form of a running commentary, for example: 'Large Church with Spire coming up on the right... We've just passed that... There's a small turnoff on the left and a wood coming up on the right... The road is turning sharp left ..., etc.'

Key skills:

- observing;
- reporting clearly, accurately, and precisely.

Grid references

All Ordnance Survey maps are covered with a grid – see the example[1] printed in this section. This aids map readers in identifying specific locations.

Four-figure grid references. The grid is numbered along the top, bottom and sides of the map. We can use the numbers to give every grid square on the map a distinct identity. For convenience they are repeated at intervals across the map, but beware of confusing the two axes. In this example, the numbers run from 76 to 80 along the top and 86 to 90 along the side. On other maps they can be anything between 00 and 99.

When identifying grid squares *always* use the numbers at the top/bottom first and the numbers along the side second.

To identify a particular square, always use the vertical line on the left of the square (identifying numbers are at the top of the map) and the horizontal line running along the bottom of the square (identifying numbers are on either side of the map). For example, grid square 7787 is so called because the vertical grid line on its left boundary is 77 and the grid line running along its bottom edge is 87.

For further practice, identify two more squares.

The above numbers are known as four-figure grid references, and are accurate to 1 kilometre (the size of each grid square). These are very useful for rough-and-ready directions.

---

[1] Based upon Ordnance Survey mapping with the permission of the controller of HMSO.

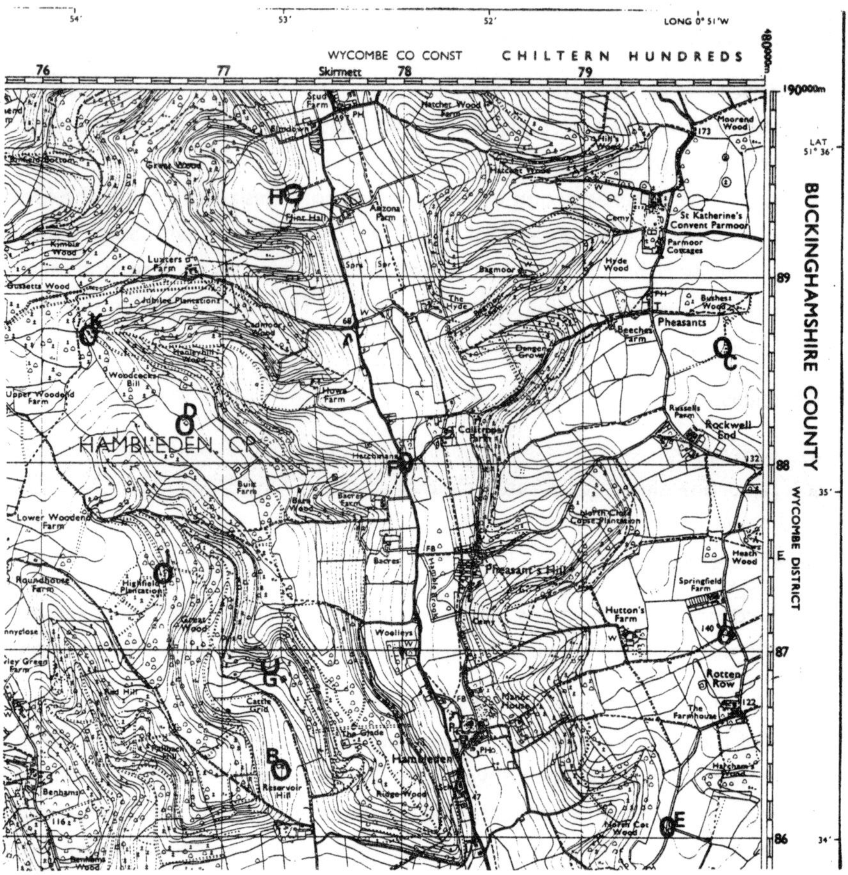

Based upon Ordnance Survey mapping with the permission of the controller of HMSO. © Crown copyright.

Six-figure grid references Four-figure grid references have their limitations. For example, if you were asked to go to the circular wood in grid square 7989 on our sample map, you would be confused because there are two in that square.

To avoid this confusion, there are 6-figure references. These are accurate to 100 metres. They are worked out by taking the 4-figure reference and breaking it down into tenths. This is often done adequately by visual estimation, but a grid referencing aid, the romer, will help accuracy. Use of the romer is explained later. For now, try visual estimation.

As a worked example, the process for working out a 6-figure grid reference appropriate for the Road Junction marked A on the map is:

Step 1: Its four figure reference is 77 88.

When carrying out the exercises on pages 282–4 of the *Outdoor Training* sourcebook, please use this map instead of the map printed on page 282. The map on page 282 is not to a common scale and cannot be used in conjunction with the Romer on page 284.

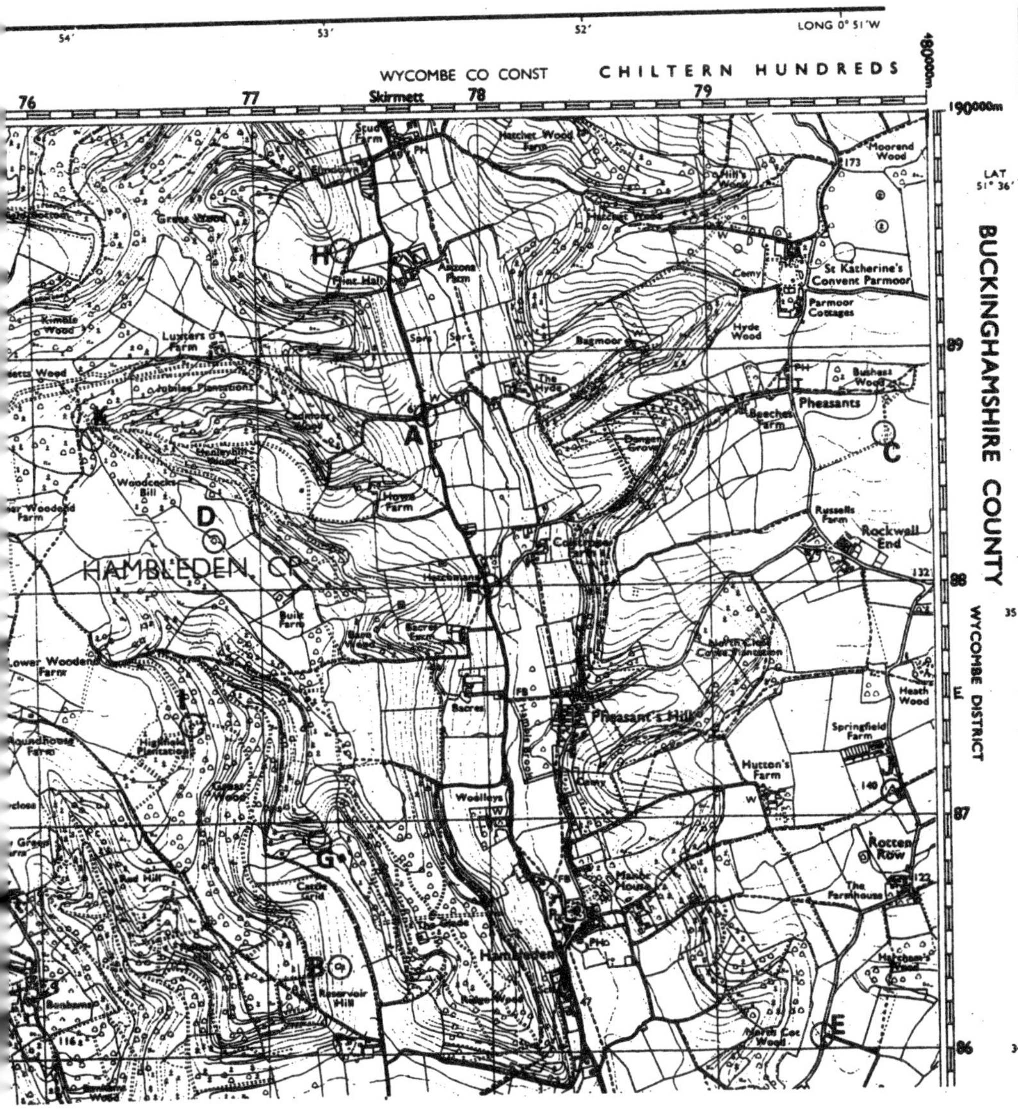

Based upon Ordnance Survey mapping with the permission of the controller of HMSO.

Step 2: It is 7 tenths (7/10) of the way from 77 to 78 and 7 tenths (7/10) of the way from 88 to 89.

This could be written as 77.7 + 88.7, but is commonly abbreviated to 777 887 or, more usually, 777887; either will do.

There are *no* five-figure references. If an object is on or very near the main grid line, the figure zero is included. Thus, on the printed map, the road junction F is at reference 780 880.

Check your understanding by working out the following examples from the map:

B – field enclosure ____________ C – bend in track ____________

D – copse ____________ E – road junction ____________

Answers
B...773 863 C...798 887
D...768 882 E...794 860

Eight-figure grid references Sometimes even six figures are not accurate enough. In this case we use an eight-figure grid reference, which is accurate to ten metres. The idea is to take the six-figure principle a step further, subdividing each tenth of a grid square into hundredths. This cannot be done adequately with the naked eye, so the romer (see below) is indispensable.

Using the romer

For the purpose of this teach-in we are working the process for finding the eight-figure reference for the wall junction G on the sample map.

You should now have a reading of 7726 8689, which is the eight-figure grid reference for point G.

Check your understanding by working out the following four examples from the map:

H – wall junction ____________ I – track junction ____________

J – track junction ____________ K – triangulation pillar ____________

Answers
H...7736 8943 I...7668 8741
J...7980 8710 K...7625 8869

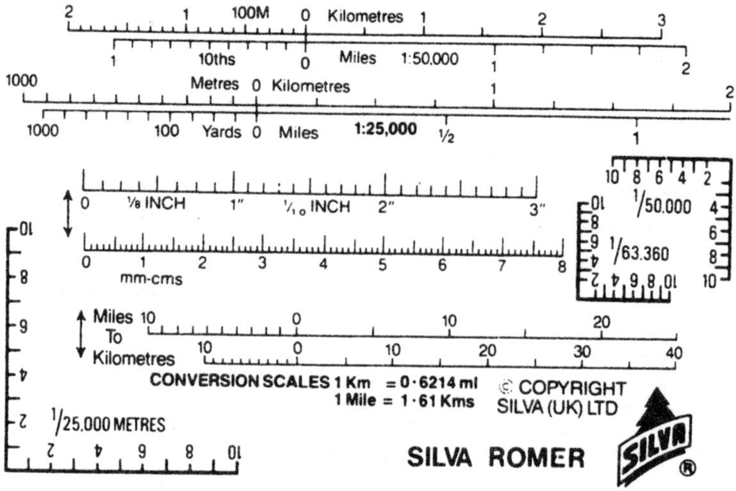

The Romer[1]

Stage	*Key point*
Step 1: Write down the four-figure reference on a scrap of paper.	Ensure there is a gap between the numbers, e.g. 77__ 86__.
Step 2: Turn the Romer upside down so that the 1:25,000 scale is on the top right.	
Step 3: Place the right-hand corner of the scale exactly on the wall junction by moving the romer.	Ensure the whole of the romer is parallel with the grid.
Step 4: Read back to the point where the vertical grid line crosses the romer and record the number (which should be something like 26, i.e. 26/100th) after the first pair on your scrap paper. This should now read 7726 86__.	Keep the romer still! Estimate tenths of each segment.
Step 5: Read down to the point where the horizontal grid line crosses the romer and record the number (which should be something like 89, i.e. 89/100th) after the second pair on your scrap of paper.	Keep the romer still! Estimate tenths of each segment.

[1] Reproduced by permission, SILVA (UK) LTD.

ENVIRONMENT AND HERITAGE

It is a sad fact that too much interaction between man and the outdoors causes damage to the environment. This is particularly true of popular areas for outdoor activities, and National Park Authorities and other bodies sometimes find themselves in the unenviable position of discouraging the use of outdoor facilities simply to avoid the destruction or degradation of rare wildlife habitats and places of beauty.

Examples of damage to the environment by outdoor activities in Britain include threats to sandstone cliff-faces through friction caused by climbing ropes, over-use of popular pathways causing serious erosion, and the vandalizing by souvenir hunters of irreplaceable rock formations in caves.

Other than the latter, these are usually innocently caused by people simply going to beautiful places without malicious intent. Nevertheless, damage is damage, and should be minimized or avoided.

Erosion is obvious, but sometimes the damage is more subtle. We know of one area in the Peak District which we had happily used for gorge-rescue exercises, securing ropes to trees in the time-honoured manner. We no longer do so because we discovered through a chance conversation that the trees were hosts to a very rare moss. Unless you are an expert, rare moss looks just the same as the stuff which makes your patio slippery in winter ... but once you know that such things exist it is extremely irresponsible to carry on endangering them.

As well as the natural environment, our man-made heritage is important to others and should be left unblemished. Groups are sometimes keen, for example, to remove artefacts from disused metal mines and should be strongly discouraged from doing so as they may well be destroying the pleasure of discovery for others and removing from context items which would otherwise be of great interest to industrial archaeologists.

In order to minimize risks to environment and heritage, we set out below guidelines for responsible use of outdoor media.

General

- Follow the Country Code. This is reproduced on a separate sheet (page 287) for issue to groups. We suggest you issue it to all at the start of every programme. It is also available free in a variety of formats from the Countryside Commission (Postal Sales Dept., PO Box 124, Walgrave, Northampton NN6 9TL) as part of the Countryside Access Charter.
- Avoid areas of known environmental sensitivity such as designated Sites of Special Scientific Interest.
- Strongly discourage behaviour likely to lead to environmental damage or historical vandalism, such as removal or harm to local flora or the purloining of apparently trivial historical artefacts.
- Be prepared to change venues at short notice as a previously useable site may have become environmentally sensitive. Examples of where we have done this include cliff-faces on which rare birds have nested and mines which have become the habitat of bats.
- Adopt a generally positive attitude to the environment.

Cliffs and rock faces

Avoid damage to these. In the more popular areas, some crags have been changed forever by over-use. Reduce this process by:

- Protecting the rope and crag – at places where they meet – with a proprietary rope protector or even a carpet sample.
- Wherever possible rigging safety and other ropes to something naturally on the site such as rocks or trees. For everyone's (and everything's!) sake, use multiple belays which will reduce the stress on any single item. This is not a book on rigging technique, but it is as well to be aware of this.
- Not using cliffs upon which birds are nesting.
- Avoiding damage to crags by bolting etc. Climbing ethics actually vary from area to area on this subject, but it is best to avoid any hint of crag-alteration by not doing it at all.
- Checking that any crags you intend to use are not – as is the case for example in some limestone crags and quarries – the site of rare plants.

Caves and mines

Caves and the rock formations within them take thousands of years to evolve. The formations can be destroyed in seconds. Mines often contain items of priceless interest to industrial archaeologists. Avoid damage by:

- Invoking 'take nothing but pictures, leave nothing at all of your own' policy in all underground locations.
- Avoiding touching formations.
- Washing off any accidental marks.
- Avoiding areas which have been taped, wired, or roped-off as these are likely to be places of particular sensitivity. Ensure qualified safety staff cordon-off sensitive places if this has not already been done.
- Never leaving litter. Take it out with you.
- Not using carbide lamps. These old caver's favourites cast a very good light but spent carbide can wreak havoc with the delicate underground ecological balance and pollute water.
- Not disturbing bats or other forms of underground life. This is best done by avoiding the appropriate locations altogether.

THE COUNTRY CODE

- Enjoy the countryside and respect its life and work
- Guard against all risks of fire
- Fasten all gates
- Keep your dogs under close control
- Keep to public paths across farmland
- Use gates and stiles to cross fences, hedges and walls
- Leave livestock, crops and machinery alone
- Take your litter home
- Help to keep all water clean
- Protect wildlife, plants and trees
- Take special care on country roads
- Make no unnecessary noise

(Used with the permission of the Countryside Commission.)

FURTHER READING

General

A useful book covering many aspects, including the basics of navigation, weather, first aid, conservation and party leadership is *Mountaincraft and Leadership* by Eric Langmuir, published by The Scottish Sports Council and the Mountainwalking Leader Training Board (1984). This manual is highly authoritative and is required reading for most mountain qualifications. It contains very practical advice on a wide range of subjects.

Access and Conservation

- *Rights of Way and Access to the Countryside* by J.F. Garner, published by Longmans (1982).
- *Countryside Conservation* by H. Hill, published by Moorland Publishing (1980).
- *Wildlife and Countryside Act*, HMSO (1981).

Navigation

There are a wide variety of books on the subject of navigation and mapreading techniques. We have found that an inexpensive, well-written, easy-to-follow introduction is *Simply Map Reading* by Richard Neve, published jointly by Telegraph Publications and Ordnance Survey (1988).

Caving/underground

Once again a wide variety of publications is available, including gazetteers of caves of the world on a country-by-country basis. The one we have found to be of most general use is: *Caving and Potholing* by David Judson and Arthur Champion, published by Granada Paperbacks (1981). This book also contains a useful further reading list covering detailed works on such subjects as Caving clubs, cave surveying, cave photography and so on.

Local caving guides are also invaluable sourcebooks. A selection for the main areas is listed below:

- *Northern Caves, Volumes 1–5* by A. and D. Brooks *et al*, published by Dalesman, Clapham, North Yorkshire, 1975 onwards.
- *Caves of Derbyshire*, T.D. Ford (ed.), published by Dalesman, various editions from 1974 onwards.
- *Caves of South Wales* by T. Stratford, Cordee (Leicester), 1978 onwards.
- *Mendip Underground –A Caver's Guide* by D.J. Irwin and Antony Knibbs, Mendip Publishing, 1987 onwards.
- *Underground in Furness* by E.G. Holland, Dalesman, 1967 onwards.

Other titles are available for areas of minor speleological interest from specialist bookshops.

Works on mining are hard to come by and usually confined to highly specific areas or even a single mine. Our advice is to buy whatever you can whenever you can –that's what we do! A useful source is the Peak District Mining Museum in Matlock Bath, which carries most titles currently available. Other mining museums are also often helpful, as are public libraries in old mining areas for loan copies of books.

Cliffs and Crags

A visit to any climbing shop will give you a wide choice of books ranging from introductory material through a multitude of local guides (similar in format to the caving guides) to highly detailed accounts of major expeditions. For general purposes and because it is a well illustrated A-to-Z guide we recommend *Climbing Terms and Techniques* by Ken Crocket, published by Patrick Stephens Ltd (1990) and reprinted (1993) in budget form by Fraser Stewart Book Wholesale Ltd., Waltham Abbey, Essex.

USEFUL ADDRESSES

Each major outdoor activity has at least one governing or co-ordinating body, the functions of which are to recommend basic standards and generally co-ordinate the activity in question. Among these are:

- The British Canoe Union, John Dudderidge House, Adbolton Lane, West Bridgeford, Nottinghamshire, NG2 5AS
- The National Caving Association, 45 Gwernyfed Avenue, Three Cocks, Brecon, Powys LD3 0RT
- The British Mountaineering Council, Crawford House, Precinct Centre, Booth Street East, Manchester M13 9RZ
- Mountaineering Council for Scotland, 1 St Colme Street, Edinburgh EH3 6AA
- The British Orienteering Federation, Riversdale, Dale Road North, Darley Dale, Matlock, Derbyshire DE4 2HX
- The Ramblers Association, 1–5 Wandsworth Road, London SW8 2XX

These organizations can provide a wealth of useful advice, information and guidelines as to what is considered good practice in the relevant activity.

Other addresses are:

- Adventure Education, 39 Brunswick Square, Penrith, Cumbria, CA11 7LS. A useful source of information, not least of which is the annual *Outdoor Source Book* which they publish and which contains a wealth of useful addresses.
- The Countryside Commission, John Dower House, Crescent Place, Cheltenham, Gloucestershire GL50 3RA (plus regional offices). There is also a Countryside Commission for Scotland with headquarters at Battleby, Redgorton, Perth PH1 3EW.
- The Mountain Leader Training Board, address as for the British Mountaineering Council. Note that there are also mountain leadership training Boards for Northern Ireland and Scotland, addresses for which can be supplied by the MLTB.
- Council for National Parks, 4 Hobart Place, London SW1W 0HY.

The 12 National Parks of England and Wales all have offices in the relevant areas, and can be invaluable in a number of ways, not least of which is giving advice on overused areas to avoid.